Read & Write across AMERICA

STUDYING THE 50 STATES THROUGH LITERATURE

Written by

M. Carol Stone

Editor: Alaska Hults
Illustrator: Corbin Hillam
Cover Illustrator: Drew Rose
Designer: Terri Lamadrid
Cover Designer: Moonhee Pak
Art Director: Tom Cochrane
Project Director: Carolea Williams

Table of Contents

Introduction

Let's take a trip across the United States! What better way is there for students to learn about the United States than to take a fictional trip to each region? This fun unit brings to life social studies and geography lessons, while promoting the reading–writing connection that builds better writers and stronger readers.

The problem that most teachers face is finding the time to immerse their students in reading and writing. After all, language arts is just one part of the elementary school curriculum. Integrating language arts with social studies provides two instructional blocks, doubling the amount of time available for reading and writing. *Read & Write across America* provides you with

• step-by-step directions to prepare and implement the unit
• ideas for learning centers
• tips for journal entries
• a page of facts and a page of annotated bibliographies for suggested literature for each state

• reproducibles—including a student state report form, travel tickets, outline maps of the United States, and a unit planner for the teacher

Read & Write across America integrates language arts and social studies. This thematic unit promotes the use of children's literature as a springboard for writing and encourages students "to live in the author's world" as they use literature to "travel" from state to state. During their journey across the states, students

• record in their literature response journals the setting, characters, and events of the literature they read as if they were actually there
• write about the climate, terrain, history, and subcultures of the states and regions they read about
• comment on actions the characters take and how the characters are affected by the events of the times in which they live
• participate in additional learning experiences through work at centers and suggested extension activities

Students learn about the traditions and idiosyncrasies of the American people in relationship to where they live. Instead of just hearing about them, they listen to the literature, and then they write about being there when the event took place. The imaginative element of this thematic unit motivates students to be active participants in their own learning and facilitates reading comprehension by building a scaffolding of experience on which to build their new learning.

Unit Overview

This thematic unit has limitless possibilities for expansion. You can spend a few months or all year on the unit, depending on your resources and time available. Initially, start by reading aloud a few books about the United States (see page 15), discussing the various regions of the United States and how they differ, and inviting the class to choose one state from each region to explore through literature set in that state. Once your class has chosen the places they will visit, assemble the materials for the first state, send home the parent letter (see page 30), and host the kickoff celebration (see page 15). Decide ahead of time which extension activities (see page 21) you will include for which states. Enlist parent volunteers to help you prepare for those activities.

As your resources and comfort level grow, add additional states and/or extension activities. You might include six states the first year and twelve the next, gradually building your unit to a level that works for your students' and your curriculum needs.

This thematic unit is not intended to take the place of an in-depth study of the fifty states, although it may be an excellent supplement to that unit. First and foremost, *Read & Write across America* is a literature unit. Its connecting theme is the intuitively motivating United States.

Most of your lessons for this thematic unit will follow this basic sequence:

• Reading
Have the whole class read one selection (as a read-aloud, as a class, in partners, small groups or individually), or assign specific books to partners or small groups of students (in literature circles) based on their reading ability. Another option is to invite students to choose a book they are interested in and read it with a partner or in a literature circle. See pages 45–143 for recommended literature for each state.

• Literature Response in Journals
Have students independently write and illustrate a journal entry. See pages 16–19 for teaching tips and ideas for journal entries.

• Learning Centers
Invite students to work independently in various centers. See pages 10–11 for ideas for each center.

• Extension Activities
Have students demonstrate or expand their knowledge of each state in one or more extension activities. See pages 21–23 for extension ideas.

State Information and Suggested Literature Pages

Pages 44–143 contain a pair of pages for each state. The left-hand page presents state information (e.g., capital, motto, bird), and the right-hand page features suggested children's literature.

The state information pages are divided into two sections. The top half of each page provides a brief list of the information students will include in their state reports. This list also serves as a handy answer key for you to check students' answers. The population numbers for each state are from Census 2000. Your students may list lower numbers if they are using resources published before the 2000 census. If you want students to use more current information, go to the U.S. Census Bureau's Web site at www.census.gov to print out a copy of the ranking table for each state. Students' information for some categories (e.g., state mottos and the names of state birds and trees) may vary slightly from what is listed because of variations in translations from the original Latin.

The bottom half of each state information page lists a few facts or trivia that you may use to spark their interest. This information is not intended to serve as an answer key for students' summaries of their state reports. Their summaries will vary depending on the resources and time they had to research the state.

The literature pages provide a list of suggested books for students to read as they study each state. Supplement this list with any other books that meet the needs of your students. Use books that are set in a particular state or books that reflect a single period of time or a single event in the history of a state. The books students read do not necessarily need to provide a great deal of factual information about each state. Students will discover much of that type of information in the learning centers you provide.

Information for State Reports

Fun Facts to Build Student Interest

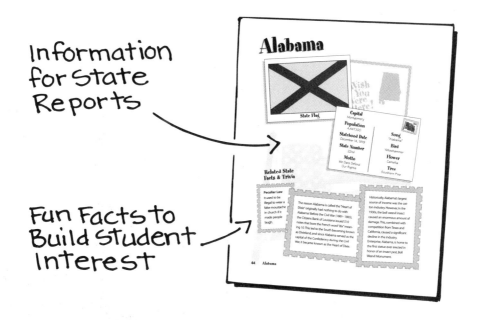

Selecting the Books

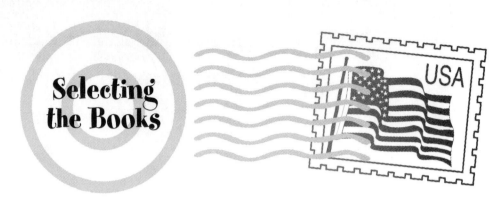

The books listed in this unit represent a wide variety of genres. Have students read books that feature different types of writing. Use the following descriptions as a guide to help you select the types of books that will work best in your classroom.

• Biography
Biographies describe the lives of famous people and often include information on their state of birth or fame.

• Cultural
Books that describe a specific subculture are often of great interest to students. They add depth to a student's understanding of the variety of people who live in a particular geographical area.

• Current Events
Books that cover current events tend to be centered around current political, social, or environmental issues particular to a region or to the country as a whole. A book on the current president, for example, is likely to have a great deal of information about the state in which he was born, raised, or served in office.

• General Fiction
Some books set in a given state or region present entirely fictional accounts. The general fiction titles recommended in this book offer either information about the location or insight into the lifestyles of some of the people who live there. All events and characters are fictitious.

• Geography
Some books, although they may tell a story, focus on the terrain, climate, and distribution of plant and animal life of a specific area.

• Historical Fiction

In these books, some of the settings, events, and characters the author describes really did happen, but details may have been invented to fill in the unknown or add to the excitement of the story.

• Historical Nonfiction

In historical nonfiction books, all events in the story are real and the author presents only known or strongly supported facts.

• Information

Many cities and states have informational picture books. These work well as introductory books to a particular state. Travel books also fall into this category.

• Legends

Legends relate cultural ideas associated with certain regions.

• Science

These books address environmental issues, the weather, plants, animals, nutrition, and other science-related subjects.

Reading-Writing Connection

Encouraging students to write can sometimes be a challenge. We aren't all natural authors, and we shouldn't expect our students to be. Inviting students to write responses to interesting and meaningful literature allows them to build on the structure and sequence of the author's work and gives them the opportunity to further develop the author's symbolism, ideas, and characters. In short, responding to literature teaches students to live in the author's world. Through their writing, students put themselves in the story. In this way, they write about what they experienced as a character within the story instead of merely telling about the story.

Students improve their reading skills through their efforts to write. They improve their decoding (word-attack) skills through word-building practice. Students increase their reading comprehension through reading literature that provides them with the schema that connects them to the story. When you read aloud books, stop at significant places to reflect, compare, question, or comment on what the author is saying or what the characters are thinking. Students will transfer this strategy to their own reading experiences. Here are other examples of how to address reading comprehension skills throughout the unit:

Decoding and word-building practice

Students will practice decoding during their reading and word-building during their writing, but they will also benefit if you take advantage of teachable moments such as these:

- After your class has brainstormed a list of words they might need for their journal writing that day (see page 16), take the opportunity to use the list to review any word-attack skills you have recently taught in your language arts program. For example, point out that some of the words contain the suffix –ly. Invite students to review the meaning of the suffix and name other words that end in –ly that would be useful for their journal writing that day.
- Challenge students to use words that are new to them in their journal entries. Refer them to the list of words they brainstormed, and challenge them to use at least one word that is new to them.
- Ask students to demonstrate a different skill each time they write in their journal. For example, ask them to include in their entries words that contain more than one syllable or use a certain number of words that have prefixes or suffixes.

Language mechanics skills

Introduce language mechanics skills in your language arts lessons, and then ask students to use specific skills in their journal entries. These skills might include

• using commas in a series or direct quotations
• demonstrating the proper way to write and punctuate city and state names
• writing a friendly letter

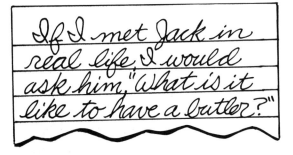

Reading comprehension and schema for literature connections

The entire unit provides opportunities to support and assess reading comprehension, but here are a few ways to provide direct support:

• Discuss journal entries that demonstrate insight into the elements of the story such as the setting, character development, or the solution of a problem.
• Before asking students to write a journal entry, provide opportunities for pairs to vocalize to each other what they read that day and their reactions to it.
• Provide visual organizers so that students may sketch out the story on webs, outlines, and flowcharts.

Comparison of or reflection on elements of fiction/nonfiction

As students read, look for opportunities to point out key elements of the story. Discuss general ideas after students complete their reading for the day, but ask students to pause during their reading to discuss specific character development or plot resolutions. Use the following examples to have students compare or reflect on elements in their reading:

• Talk to students when something crucial is happening in the story, and ask them if they can relate to how the character must feel or if anything like what is happening to the character has happened to them.
• Ask students to compare the feelings of two characters who face similar problems. Have them discuss how the characters' feelings are the same and how they are different.
• When a character solves a problem, ask students to reflect silently on how the character chose to act. Then, invite them to share their thoughts with the class. Then, have students compare this resolution with that of another character in the same story or a similar story with a different character.

Learning Centers

Design centers around specific themes, holidays, or geographic features of the state the class is studying. For example, when the class studies Louisiana, set up an art center where students can make Mardi Gras masks. Generic centers such as the ones listed below can be easily adapted to each state:

- Listening Center—Provide headphones, a tape player, and a variety of books on tapes, including books being read by the class or promotional materials from travel agencies or state tourism agencies.
- Library Center—Stock the class library with additional books that are set in the state the class is studying, as well as books about or set in other states in the same region. Encourage students to use the information they learn in these books in their journal entries. This is a great place for those series of books that have background information about each state. Here are just a few:

America the Beautiful series
(Children's Press)

From Sea to Shining Sea series
(Children's Press)

Hello USA series
(Lerner Communications Company)

Portrait of America series
(Raintree/Steck Vaughn)

One Nation series
(Bridgestone Books)

- Computer Center—Have students use the computer to research some of the state information (see page 5 for the URL for the most up-to-date census information) or to write up the information that they discover. In advance, locate and bookmark the Web sites you wish them to explore. Have students use the bookmarks to navigate the Internet. This is also an excellent center for an adult volunteer to supervise.

• Discovery Center—Provide jigsaw puzzles, word games such as crossword puzzles, maps (especially topographic), and other materials for students to explore at their own pace. Also provide atlases, encyclopedias, and books on the various states for students to use for their state reports (see page 20).

• Math Center—Provide research material, and challenge students to find data on each state in the region they are studying. Challenge them to find

  • cities with the greatest and least populations

  • destinations with the highest and lowest elevations

  • areas with the greatest and least rainfall

  • distances between two locations

Once students have gathered the information, have them calculate comparisons for each state in the region. For example, once students have found the cities with the greatest and least populations for each state in the region, have them calculate the differences in population between two or more of those locations. Alternatively, have them research changes in population for a specific state over time.

• Bookmaking—Have students use materials from the Library or Discovery Center to make simple books that compare information they have gathered. Have a list of different kinds of books students may work on. For example, while the class studies Louisiana, have students make a book that compares the smaller ecosystems of that state (e.g., bayou, wetlands, urban). For a final project, have students compare the characteristics of each of the six regions of the United States. (See page 12 for the breakdown of each region.)

Alaska, California, Hawaii, Oregon, Washington.

The Pacific Coast States

The Rocky Mountain States

The Southwestern States

The Midwestern States

The Southern States

The Northeastern States

The number of centers you set up will vary according to the time you have available, your resources, and the size of your class. Start with two centers and add more as needed.

Preparing for the Trip

1. Decide on the itinerary

Give each student a map of Regions of the United States (page 28), and show students the regions of the United States on a large wall map. Have students use a different color crayon or marker to fill in each region. Decide in advance how many states you want to cover in the unit, and share this information with the class. Be sure to tell students that they will read a variety of fiction and nonfiction books set in each state they "visit" and will complete some independent investigation into the history and current events of each state. Invite the class to choose from each region the states they wish to visit together. Have them keep in mind the total number of states you wish to include, begin with their home state, and include at least one state from each region. Collect the colored maps from students, and add them to their travel packets (see page 14). After the class has chosen the states to visit, begin collecting books for each of those states. The regions are as follows:

Northeastern States
Connecticut
Maine
Massachusetts
New Hampshire
New Jersey
New York
Pennsylvania
Rhode Island
Vermont

Southern States
Alabama
Arkansas
Delaware
Florida
Georgia
Kentucky
Louisiana
Maryland
Mississippi
North Carolina
South Carolina
Tennessee
Virginia
West Virginia

Midwestern States
Illinois
Indiana
Iowa
Kansas
Michigan
Minnesota
Missouri
Nebraska
North Dakota
Ohio
South Dakota
Wisconsin

Southwestern States
Arizona
New Mexico
Oklahoma
Texas

Rocky Mountain States
Colorado
Idaho
Montana
Nevada
Utah
Wyoming

Pacific Coast States
Alaska
California
Hawaii
Oregon
Washington

2. Gathering materials

Gather the books you need for the first state (your home state), atlases and encyclopedias, and any materials you need for the learning centers. Have each student bring in a spiral notebook to use as a writing journal. Prepare a travel packet (see page 14) for each student. Display a large U.S. map on one wall of your classroom. To make your own map, copy the United States Outline Map (page 29) onto an overhead transparency. Cover a wall with butcher paper, and then project the transparency onto the wall. Use a marker to trace the map on the butcher paper. Label each state, or use tagboard and tape to make a label for each state . Ask students to take turns placing each label on the map as a classroom activity at the start of the unit.

3. Send home a parent letter

Involve parents in the planning by sending home the letter on page 30. Parents are a tremendous resource for this unit, and having their support will enable you to build in more of the extension activities (see pages 21–25).

4. Assemble the travel packets

Use pocket folders to create a travel packet for each student. Include each student's completed map of the Regions of the United States (see page 12), a spiral bound notebook for use as a travel journal, an assembled travel passport (see directions below), and copies of the Travel Tickets (pages 32–39).

To create a travel passport, make several double-sided copies of the Travel Passport (page 31) for each student. (Students will need one travel ticket for each state they visit throughout the unit; the reproducible has room for four travel tickets.) Staple each student's set of pages to the center of a piece of blue construction paper, and fold the paper in half to make a "passport." Make copies of the Travel Tickets (pages 32–39) students will need for the states in each region they study. (Throughout the unit, have students color and cut out the travel ticket for the state they are studying and then glue it in their passport book.) As an alternative, give students a sticker that relates to each state

(e.g., corn for Iowa, chili pepper for Arizona) instead of a travel ticket. Or, have students research each state's seal and draw it in their passport book.

All Aboard!

1. Read aloud a general USA book

Read an introductory book about the United States to whet students' interest in the unit, giving them some background knowledge about the geography and beauty of the country. Then explain to students that they will be taking an imaginative "trip" through each region of the United States by reading various pieces of literature set in each region. Here are some suggested titles for the introductory book:

> *America: My Land, Your Land, Our Land*
> by W. Nikola-Lisa (Lee & Low Books)

> *Purple Mountain Majesties*
> by Barbara Younger (Dutton)

> *The Scrambled States of America*
> by Laurie Keller (Henry Holt and Company)

> *This Land Is Your Land*
> by Woody Guthrie (Little, Brown & Company)

Place additional books, such as those listed on pages 42–43, in your class library.

2. Celebrate your departure

Host a bon voyage party for students. Invite parents to come for the celebration. Take pictures of them with their children in front of the U.S. map. Use the party to give an overview of the unit. Display some of the books students will read, and introduce each learning center. Invite parents to contribute items such as travel souvenirs to the Discovery Center and any materials you may need for planned extension activities. Also, invite other school personnel such as principals, school secretaries, custodians, librarians, and nurses. School personnel will provide a new audience for your students' enthusiasm, which is especially important if some parents are unable to attend.

3. Hand out travel packets to students

Invite students to review their trip "documents" (i.e., passport, travel tickets, travel journal, U.S. map). Have them write *(student's name)'s Passport* on the cover of their passport.

The Basic Itinerary

For each state that the class visits, the core activities will be reading books set in that state, reflecting on the reading, and then writing about it. At the start of each "visit" with a state, have them begin by marking their passports. The next few pages outline the details for each of these steps:

1. Start the trip

Have students take out their travel packet and remove the ticket for their state. (See alternative suggestions on page 14.) Ask them to color the ticket and glue it in the first box of their passport. Remind students that their purpose for reading is to learn about the people, history, culture, and climate of the state that is the setting of the book.

2. Read the book

Begin by introducing key vocabulary. For example, in books about the migration west, define the terms *prairie schooner* and *running meat* before students begin reading. Then, as you read, point out the appearance of key terms. Have students listen carefully for context clues that further explain each term. Read the story (or chapter) in its entirety, so that students may savor the story line. Then, discuss with students specific topics to clarify ideas. Discuss references to processes, jobs, food, and travel that are historical in nature or reveal information about the state or region that is the setting of the book.

Illustrations can provide helpful clues. Point them out in the literature as you come to them. Often, the illustrations hold meaningful infor-mation that is instrumental to the story. Ask students about pertinent story details that are shown in the illustrations. Students will include these details in their journal illustrations and their journal entries.

3. Assign the journal entry

Have students respond to the reading each day. When you first begin this thematic unit, model your expectation for a journal entry. As you write on the board or overhead projector, think aloud so that students can follow the development of your entry. Adapt the length of the entry to the fluency level of your students. The journal entry you model should show use of imagination and demonstrate that you have connected personally to the piece of literature (resulting in increased reading comprehension).

Here is an example of a journal entry for *Samson, the Hot Tub Bear* by Wendy Tokuda (Roberts Rinehart):

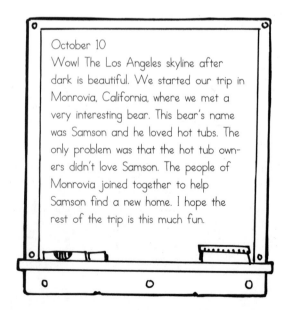

October 10
Wow! The Los Angeles skyline after dark is beautiful. We started our trip in Monrovia, California, where we met a very interesting bear. This bear's name was Samson and he loved hot tubs. The only problem was that the hot tub owners didn't love Samson. The people of Monrovia joined together to help Samson find a new home. I hope the rest of the trip is this much fun.

Ask students to remove their travel journal (spiral notebook) from their travel packet. Have students copy your entry in their travel journal and then add their own comments. After students are comfortable with this method, write only the first sentence or two. Your entry could look like this:

October 15
San Francisco even looks interesting. With the steep streets and climbing cable cars, it is so different from Los Angeles.

Have students copy the sentences and then write the rest of their journal entry. Finally, ask students to write the entire journal entry without a prompt. With more fluent students, this time will come sooner than with less fluent ones.

Before you ask students to write and illustrate their journal entries, discuss that day's reading with them. Focus the discussion on the events of the story, how it made them feel, and what they liked or didn't like. Steer them away from an impersonal story summary. As the discussion progresses, write on the board key vocabulary terms that students use in the discussion to help spark ideas when students write their own literature responses. This word bank gives students a reference for correctly spelled terms and serves as a prompt for students.

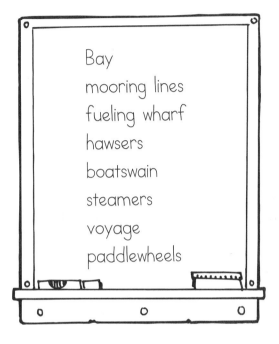

Bay
mooring lines
fueling wharf
hawsers
boatswain
steamers
voyage
paddlewheels

Do not be discouraged if students' initial journal entries do not seem very exciting. Many students are not accustomed to open-topic writing. As this thematic unit progresses and you model the use of descriptive and imaginative language, their entries will expand to reflect the improvement in their reading and writing skills.

If you do find that initially your less fluent students need some questions to get them going, give them some of the open-ended journal prompts on pages 18–19. If you display the prompts on the board or an overhead projector, make it clear to students that they do not have to write to the prompt and may write about any aspect of their literary journey that they wish.

One way to help students write more meaningful journal entries is to talk about the next state they will visit at least a day before they start reading about it. Make comments such as *I hope it won't be too hot when we are in Utah. There is a lot of desert terrain there* or *I can't wait to see the beautiful red rocks in the Utah desert.* Whenever possible, share with students your personal experiences as they relate to the stops on the trip. For instance, you might say *When I was a little girl, my family traveled through Utah. We slept under the stars. In the morning, my dad cooked pancakes for us right there in the desert.* These personal anecdotes help students anticipate a visit to the desert in Utah and will help them begin to form questions for themselves about Utah. These questions form scaffolding for their understanding as they read the literature set in Utah, which will make for more meaningful journal entries. (If you have no personal anecdotes about a state, use some of the fun trivia and state facts from the state information pages that begin on page 44.)

Open-Ended Journal Prompts

Invite less fluent students to respond to open-ended journal prompts. Insert an actual character name where "character" is italicized in the following questions. Replace other italicized text with the specific story elements as indicated:

1. Would you be insulted or complimented if someone said you were like

    A. *Character One*
    B. *Character Two*
    C. *Character Three*

   Tell which response you would have for each character and explain your answers.

2. Imagine that *Character A* could write a letter to *Character B*. Write a letter from *Character A* just after *key moment early in story*. Then write a second letter after *resolution of that incident.*

3. Draw a circle that fills the page. Divide the circle into five equal sections. In each section, write five sentences about one of the following topics: the setting, the main characters, the main problem the characters face, the most important moment in the story, and how the story ends.

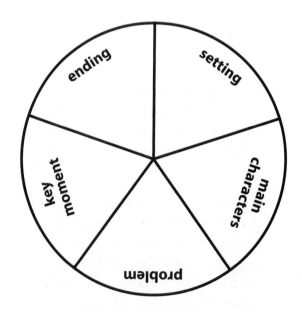

4. Make a chart of the similarities between the major and minor characters.

5. Write a lost and found ad for an object, an animal, or a person in the story.

6. Write a short statement to prove that there is both good and bad in two main characters from the story. Then decide which character is your favorite and explain your reasons.

7. This story is fictional. How is it like an event in your life that really happened?

8. Write three questions about the place where the story occurs. Research the answers and record them.

9. Write a diary entry for your character at the beginning of the story. Write one for the end of the story. Be sure your second entry shows what your character has learned from the events of the story.

10. Put yourself in *Character A's* shoes. What food did you eat and drink today? How much work did you have to do to get that food? Now think about your real life. Do you ever eat those foods? How does the way that *Character A* got his or her food compare to what you normally have to do to get food?

11. Put yourself in *Character A's* shoes. What items did you travel with today? What was the purpose of each item? In your real life, what would you normally pack for a trip? How does that compare to the items *Character A* travels with?

12. What part of today's reading was least clear to you? Make a list of questions you still have about the story. Share your finished list with *Teacher's name*.

13. Complete each sentence based on today's reading:
I learned _____.
I discovered _____.
I was surprised _____.
I'm beginning to wonder _____.
I now realize _____.
I want to find out more about _____.

Additional Excursions

As time and resources permit, you will want to add some additional opportunities for learning to your thematic unit. You may add some additional excursions, such as the research report, to each state you visit. You may add others, such as the investigation into state foods, to only a few states.

Research Report

Assign the research report at the beginning of each stop in a state or as an extension activity at the end of the unit. If you assign it as an extension activity, have a random drawing to determine which state each student will research.

Give each student a State Report reproducible (page 40). Have students use student atlases and bound or electronic encyclopedias (e.g., Encarta) to complete their research form. Ask them to summarize the highlights of what they learned during their visit to that state on the bottom of the form. Encourage students to use their travel journal to help them remember what they did and who they met when they visited the state.

Have students draw an outline of the state on a piece of drawing paper and color it in. Give each student a large piece of colored construction paper, and have students glue their report and state outline side by side on the construction paper. Display the finished reports on a bulletin board.

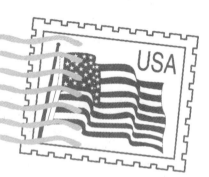

Extension Activities

Select one or all of the activities listed on pages 21–25 for students to complete during each visit to a state or region. For example, have students write postcards with one state and sample meals and snacks for another state.

Postcard Activity

Collect blank postcards from friends or parents, or have students write to a chamber of commerce in a city of the state they are studying. Or, invite students to design their own postcard on the Postcard reproducible (page 41).

Have students write postcards to their parents as if they were writing from that state. For example, when the class is visiting Plymouth, Massachusetts, have students write postcards to their parents from Plimoth Plantation. (For more information on Plymouth, visit the Plimoth Plantation Web site at www.plimoth.org.) Have students address the cards before you mail them. Here is an example of a student-written message:

This activity gives students the opportunity to practice letter-writing techniques, stay excited about the trip, and involve their parents. After their parents have enjoyed the cards, have students bring them to school and put them in their travel packets as souvenirs.

Meals and Snacks

Food is a sensory connector that links geography to the taste buds. In addition to being fun, an activity like this really makes students think about the lifestyles of the people who live in different areas.

Enlist the support of parents in preparing the meals and snacks enjoyed during the unit. Many parents are very comfortable with assisting in this way even when the menu item is unfamiliar to them. Another good source of help in this area is school and district personnel. One of the special education aides at my school cooks enchiladas for my entire class every year. I invite her to every meal or snack we have.

Alternatively, instead of actually preparing the meals, assign students the task of researching and recording a common food item or recipe for that state. Here is an example of Helen's Oklahoma discovery:

Helen Harrington
Room 12
January 21

Oklahoma Deep Fried Pickles
Makes 4 servings

Ingredients
- 1 c. buttermilk
- 3/4 t. cayenne pepper
- 2 eggs
- 2 1/4 c. all-purpose flour (divided)
- 1/4 t. garlic powder
- 1/4 t. seasoning salt
- 1/2 t. Tabasco® sauce
- 1 T. Worcestershire sauce
- 1 c. cornmeal
- 3/4 t. black pepper
- 1 t. salt
- 1 c. vegetable oil for deep frying
- deep fryer or pot
- 1 32-ounce jar of dill pickle slices
- salt and pepper

Directions
1. In a large bowl, mix buttermilk, cayenne pepper, eggs, 1/4 cup flour, garlic powder, seasoning salt, Tabasco sauce, and Worcestershire sauce.
2. In another bowl mix cornmeal, 2 cups flour, black pepper, and salt.
3. Preheat oil in a deep fryer or pot to 365°F.
4. Dip pickles into the milk mixture, and then roll them in the flour mix. Deep-fry the pickles until golden brown. Drain on paper towels. Salt and pepper to taste.

State Foods

Here are some examples of meals and snacks that originate in or are claimed by each of the states. Your students may know of others to add to the list. Products that are also grown or produced by the state are italicized.

Alabama
• corncob jelly
• red beans and rice
• pecan pie

Alaska
• *salmon*
• *caribou*
• muktuk (whale blubber)

Arizona
• Navajo taco
• salsa
• *jalapeños*

Arkansas
• *rice*

California
• sushi
• *raisins*
• *artichokes*

Colorado
• green chili
• *cantaloupe*
• *onion*

Connecticut
• New England squash pie

Delaware
• *watermelon*
• *chicken*

Florida
• *oranges*
• key lime pie

Georgia
• *peaches*
• *vidalia onions*
• Brunswick stew
• peanut brittle

Hawaii
• poi
• *pineapple*

Idaho
• *potatoes*
• *peanuts*

Illinois
• horseshoes (cheese sauce over fries and meat, all on top of toast)

Indiana
• *corn*
• *soybeans*
• *blueberries*

Iowa
• guinea grinders (hot sausage and sauce, peppers, onions, and cheese on a bun)

Kansas
• *wheat*

Kentucky
- cheese garlic grits
- baked possum
- smashed sweet potatoes
- derby pie (pecan pie with chocolate chips and a scoop of whipped cream or ice cream)
- kentucky burgoo (a stew-like dish especially popular around Kentucky Derby time)

Louisiana
- gumbo
- red beans and rice
- king cake
- po'boys (French bread stuffed with one or more of the following: roast beef, fried seafood, hot sausage, hamburger, or potato, and dressed with mayonnaise, lettuce, tomato, and pickle)

Maine
- lobster
- blueberries

Maryland
- crab cakes

Massachusetts
- clam chowder
- baked beans
- codfish

Michigan
- pasties (meat pies)
- cucumber soup
- cherries

Minnesota
- wild rice
- lutefisk (dried cod steeped in lye)
- walleye
- lefse (potato pancakes)

Mississippi
- turnips
- fried green tomatoes

Missouri
- cabbage chowder
- crayfish étouffée

Montana
- huckleberries

Nebraska
- runza (type of sandwich)
- corn
- beef

Nevada
- mutton

New Hampshire
- frappe (type of milk shake)

New Jersey
- tomatoes

New Mexico
- chili peppers
- fry bread

New York
- buffalo wings
- thin crust pizza
- bagels

North Carolina
- barbecue pork (served on a bun with cole slaw)

North Dakota
- sugar beets (food, but also a major white sugar producer)

Ohio
- buckeyes (balls of peanut butter, butter, and sugar dipped in chocolate)
- squash

Oklahoma
- fried pickles
- corn bread and pinto beans
- chicken fried steak

Oregon
- hazelnuts
- salmon

Pennsylvania
- shoofly pie
- funnel cakes
- perogies

Rhode Island
- dynamites (variety of sloppy joe)
- coffee milk (coffee syrup and milk)

South Carolina
- roasted corn and bacon relish
- roasted curried pecans

South Dakota
- buffalo burgers

Tennessee
- gritted corn bread
- spoon bread

Texas
- chili
- barbecued beef

Utah
- fry sauce (a mix of mayonnaise, ketchup, or barbeque sauce on french fries)
- Jell-O® dishes (largest Jell-O® consumption in country)

Vermont
- maple syrup and sugar

Virginia
- ham biscuits
- peanut soup

Washington
- coffee
- apples
- clams
- salmon

West Virginia
- fauter beans
- pickled corn

Wisconsin
- cheese

Wyoming
- lamb

Cookbooks

Cookbooks tend to go out of print faster than some other genres. If the following titles are not available, ask your reference librarian to help you find replacement titles:

- *The Taste of American Place: A Reader on Regional and Ethnic Foods* edited by Barbara G. Shortridge (Rowman & Littlefield)

- *The American Table: More than 400 Recipes That Make Accessible for the First Time the Full Richness of American Regional Cooking* by Ronald Johnson (Truck Press)

- *Taste of Home Magazine*—Each month they choose a state and feature a food and recipes from that state. Look for past issues at your library.

Memories from the Trip

The following activities serve as a visual reminder of the work students have completed and as a visual summary of some of what they have learned. The bulletin board activity can be completed by small groups of students with your supervision. The scrapbook should be completed with adult assistance.

Bulletin Board Ideas

Students love to see their work displayed in the classroom. Several times throughout the unit, have students do a process writing activity (e.g., brainstorm, draft, edit, revise, publish) for one of their state visits. Select a state that will allow students to produce creative artwork along with creative writing.

Students tend to be particularly motivated to put together bulletin boards that depict areas that are different from where they live. For example, New York City is a very exciting place, and students love to visit there. Skyscrapers, heavy traffic on streets, rooftop gardens, plants in window boxes, and plants on fire escapes are very intriguing to students who don't live in a city. They are eager to write and illustrate stories about visiting New York City. Have students make signs for places such as Times Square, Broadway, 42nd Street, Fifth Avenue, and Central Park, and hang them on the bulletin board with their stories.

Students who do live in cities are anxious to make bulletin board displays of wide-open spaces. Students who write stories about states in the Rocky Mountain region illustrate them with pictures of horses and cowboys. Next, invite students to make construction paper plants and animals to scatter throughout the bulletin board. A mountain range makes a striking backdrop.

Have students work in groups to complete one part of a bulletin board for a state in each region they study.

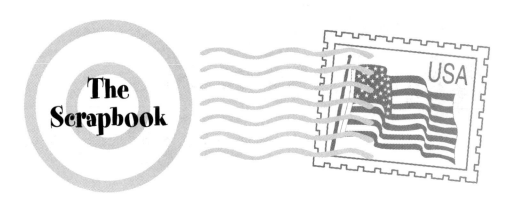

The Scrapbook

Document the class's travels by creating a scrapbook of their trip. Take photos of the students as they "travel" to each destination. Place the photos in a class scrapbook. Write a caption for each photo, or have students take turns writing the captions on a page of photos. The writing that accompanies the photos will have as much value to students and parents who view the scrapbook as the photos themselves.

Periodically, send parents an itinerary. Ask students to bring in items to share with the class. Ask parents to help their children find items at home that relate to the state they are studying. Have students hold the item they brought in to share and stand in front of the U.S. map or the bulletin board display, and take photos of them.

Ask parents to help in the assembly of the scrapbook. Develop the pictures, and then invite parent volunteers to work with small groups of students to assist them with cutting the pictures with craft scissors and mounting them in the scrapbook. Have students add memorabilia such as postcards or an outline drawing of the state. This is an ongoing project. Have volunteers complete a page or two after students visit each destination. Display the finished scrapbook at Open House.

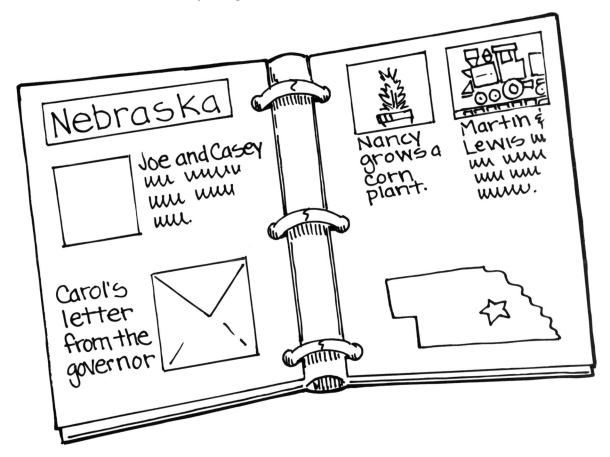

Regions of the United States

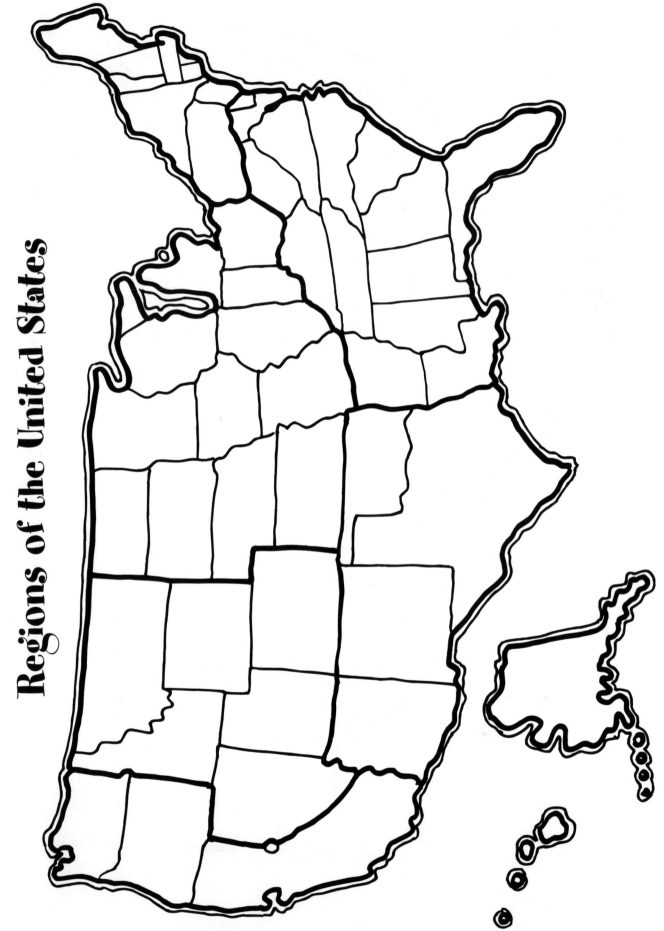

United States Outline Map

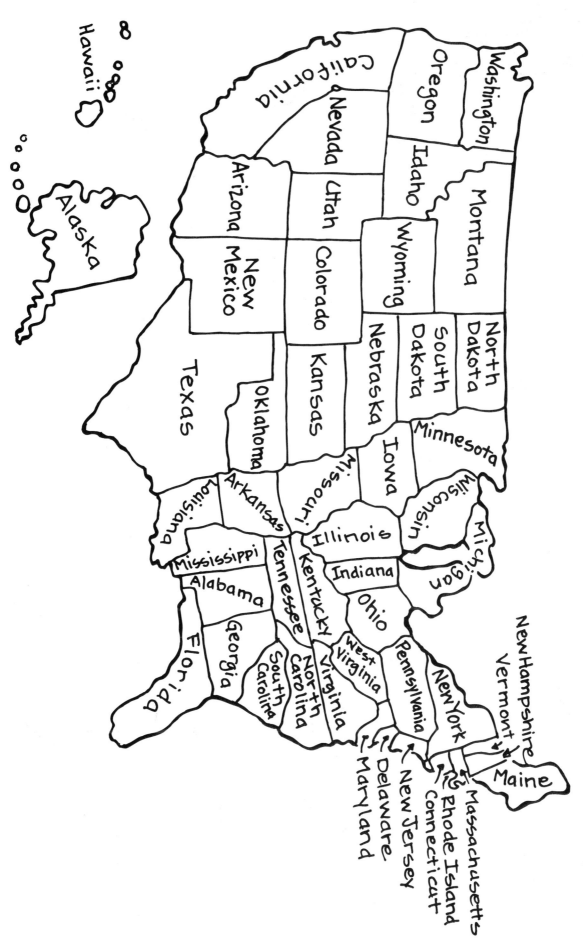

_____

Dear Parents,

Our class is preparing to embark on an imaginative trip. Students will be traveling across America . . . through their reading of children's literature. Each student will record the events of our trip in a travel journal. These journals will be keepsakes and will give students an opportunity to organize their thoughts on paper. The literature and the classroom discussion will be springboards for writing. Be sure to ask your child about his or her travels.

Please let me know if you have any items to contribute to our trip. Photos, postcards, or souvenirs related to any states would be appreciated. Clearly labeled items will be returned at the end of the unit.

Sincerely,

Travel Passport

Travel Passport

Travel Tickets

Northeastern States

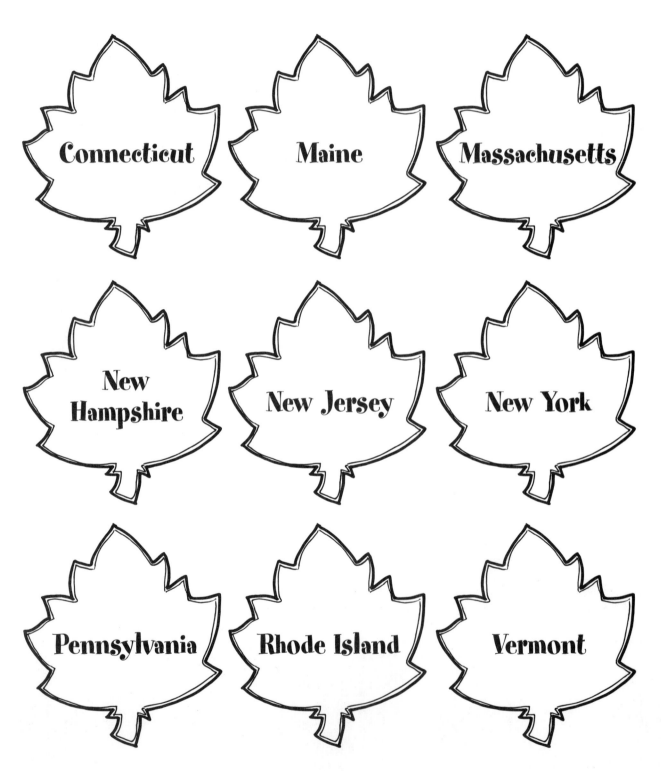

Travel Tickets

Southern States

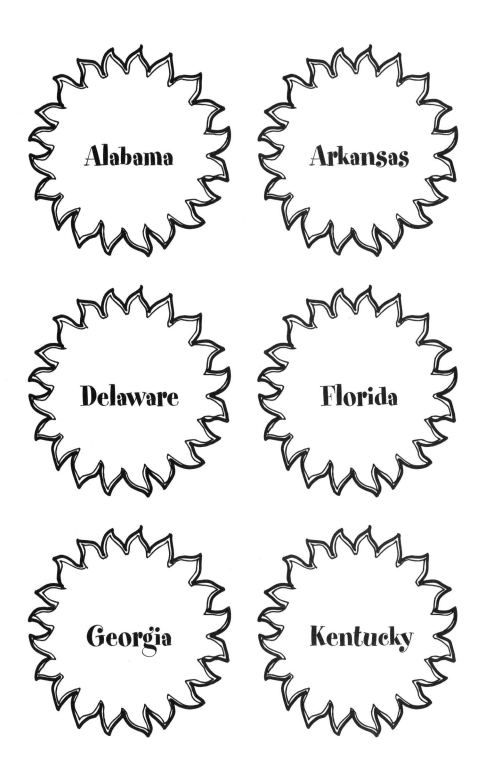

Alabama

Arkansas

Delaware

Florida

Georgia

Kentucky

Travel Tickets

Southern States (continued)

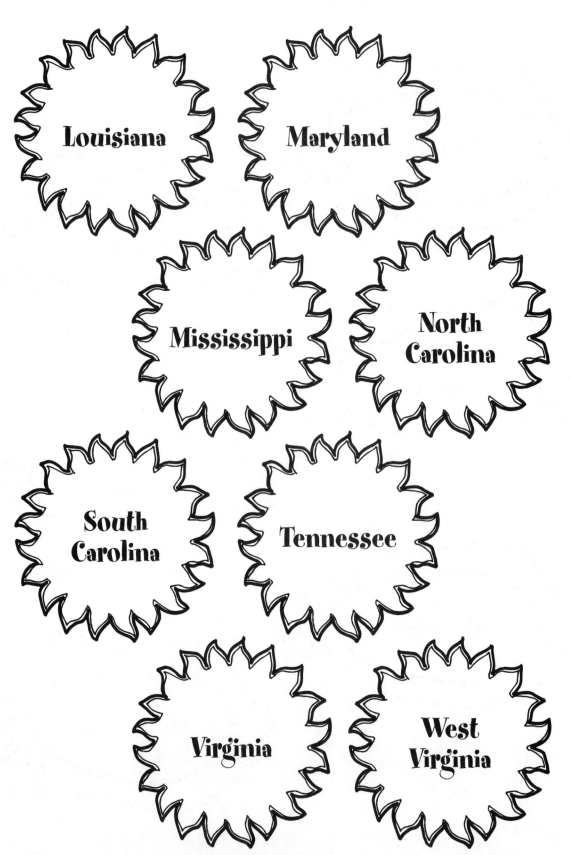

Louisiana

Maryland

Mississippi

North Carolina

South Carolina

Tennessee

Virginia

West Virginia

Travel Tickets

Midwestern States

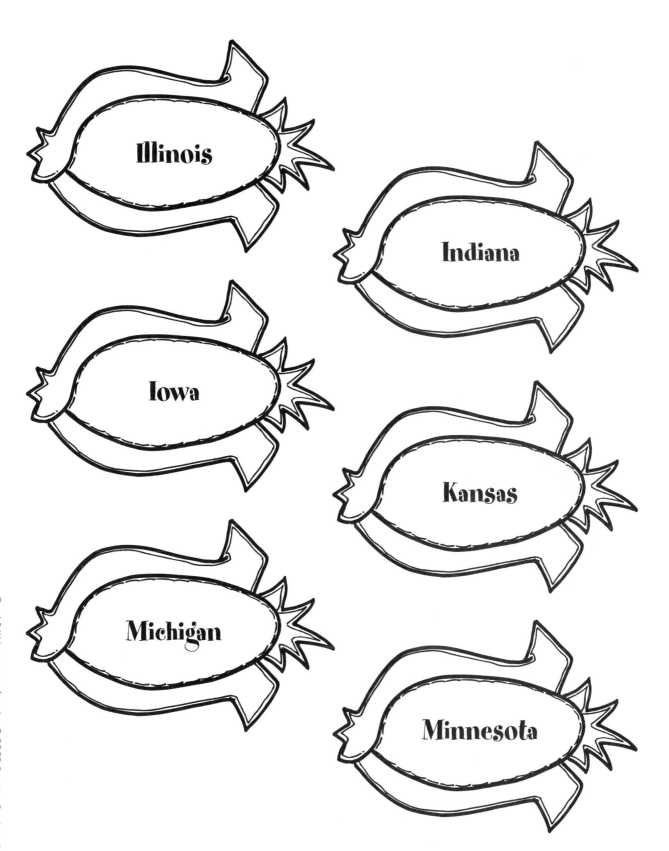

Illinois

Indiana

Iowa

Kansas

Michigan

Minnesota

Travel Tickets

Midwestern States (continued)

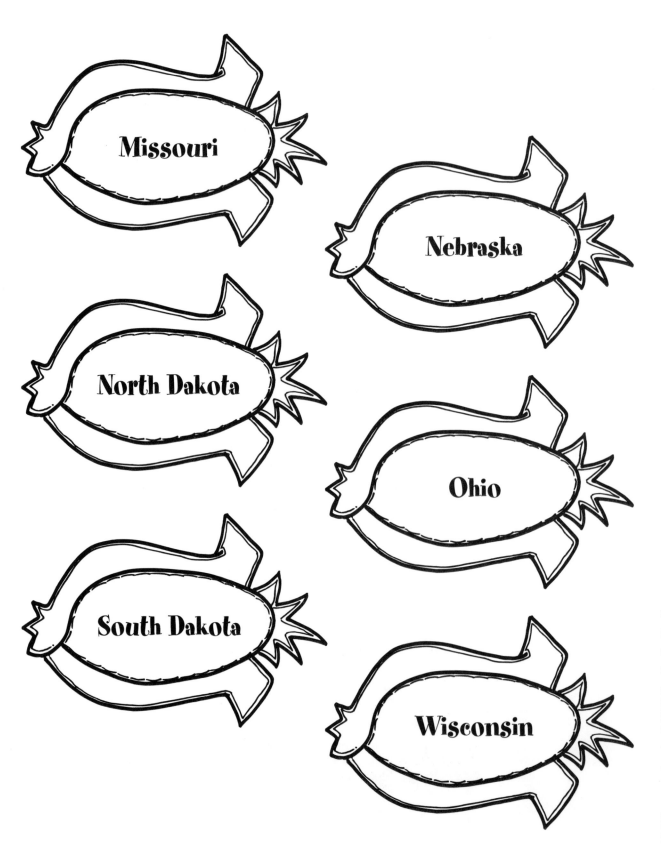

Missouri

Nebraska

North Dakota

Ohio

South Dakota

Wisconsin

Travel Tickets

Southwestern States

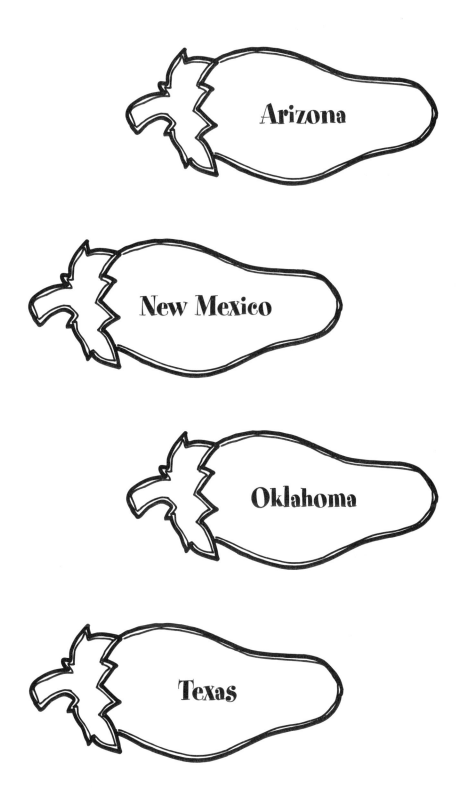

Arizona

New Mexico

Oklahoma

Texas

Travel Tickets

Rocky Mountain States

Colorado

Idaho

Montana

Nevada

Utah

Wyoming

Read & Write across America © 2002 Creative Teaching Press

Travel Tickets

Pacific Coast States

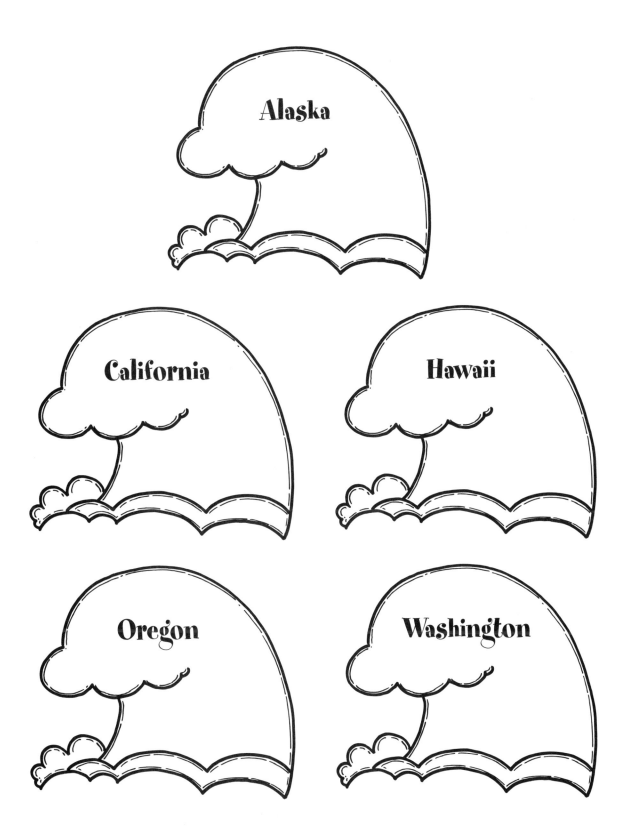

Alaska

California

Hawaii

Oregon

Washington

Name ______________________ Date ______________________

State ______________________

Capital: ______________________

Population: ______________________

Statehood Date: ______________________

State Number: ______________________

Motto: ______________________

Song: ______________________

Bird: ______________________

Flower: ______________________

Tree: ______________________

State Flag

Summarize your findings about the state.

Postcard

Create an illustration for the front of your state postcard.

Write a message on the back of your postcard according to your teacher's directions. Address your message to a friend, classmate, or parent.

Place
Stamp
Here

The United States of America

These books examine an aspect of the U.S. They can be used to stimulate interest throughout the unit or placed in a Library or Discovery Center. The ◎≋ indicates the genre of the book (see pages 6–7 for more information).

A is for America
by Devin Scillian
(Sleeping Bear Press)

This book claims to be "An American Alphabet," and it is that plus so much more. Each letter of the alphabet is represented on a beautifully illustrated page. On one side is a poem containing various "American" places, people, and things that start with that letter. On the other side of the two-page spread is a short statement that gives information about the contents of the poem. ◎≋ **Information**

Across America, I Love You
by Christine Loomis
(Hyperion Books
for Students)

This book takes the reader across the country and across the generations. Beautifully and uniquely illustrated, the book travels across the landscape of America from west to east. ◎≋ **Information**

**America: My Land,
Your Land, Our Land**
by W. Nikola-Lisa
(Lee & Low Books)

A lyrical text, accompanied by bold illustrations, depicts the contrasting characteristics of the land and the people that make up America. ◎≋ **Information**

Celebrate the 50 States
by Loreen Leedy
(Holiday House)

Each page contains maps and facts about two states. In addition to facts and bits of historical interest, there is a question about each state. The answers to the questions are provided at the back of the book. ◎≋ **Information**

**Home: A Journey
Through America**
illustrated by Thomas Locker
(Harcourt)

Thirteen poets contributed to this collection of poems that describe their homes across America. ◎≋ **Information (Poetry)**

**My America: A Poetry
Atlas of the United States**
by Bennett Hopkins
(Simon & Schuster)

This collection of poetry divides the U.S. into seven geographical regions. The book also features a section on the nation's capital. Each section contains a map, state facts, and poetry. A note from the artist explains how the paintings were done specifically to accompany each poem. ◎≋ **Geography (Poetry)**

O Beautiful for Spacious Skies
edited by Sara Boyers
(Chronicle Books)

The words to the famous poem by Katharine Lee Bates combined with beautiful illustrations make this book perfect for classroom use. This book also includes short biographies of the author of the poem and the illustrator. ◎≈ **Information**

Purple Mountain Majesties, The Story of Katharine Lee Bates and America the Beautiful
by Barbara Younger
(N A L)

As the title suggests, this book is the story of Katharine Lee Bates and the trip from Massachusetts to Colorado, in 1893, that inspired her to write the poem "America the Beautiful." The book is very nicely organized and illustrated. ◎≈ **Historical Nonfiction**

Rand McNally Student's Atlas of the United States
(Rand McNally)

Maps and state emblems in an easy-to-use format make this atlas perfect for students who are working on state reports. ◎≈ **Information**

The Scrambled States of America
by Laurie Keller
(Henry Holt & Company)

This is a hilarious story about the states, at a dinner party, deciding to switch places with each other. The result is quite funny. For example, Florida and Minnesota, who change places, both have big problems. Florida is freezing, and Minnesota is roasting and getting a terrible sunburn. ◎≈ **General Fiction**

This Land Is Your Land
Words and Music by
Woody Guthrie
(Little, Brown & Company)

The words to Woody Guthrie's well-known folk song are accompanied by paintings by Kathy Jakobsen. Hidden in small boxes in the corners of many of the pages are little bits of wisdom or observations made by Guthrie regarding his trip across the country. At the back of the book is a short biography of Guthrie's life and a very touching tribute to Guthrie by Pete Seeger, in which he shares that Guthrie wrote this song in February 1940, as he hitchhiked from Los Angeles to New York City. ◎≈ **Information**

The United States of America: A State-by-State Guide
by Millie Miller
and Cyndi Nelson
(Scholastic)

Each page has a colored map of one of the 50 states. Each map comes with information about the state's people, places, birds, flowers, and animals. This easy-to-use research book also includes a page for the nation's capital. ◎≈ **Information**

Alabama

State Flag

Wish You Were Here!

Capital
Montgomery

Population
4,447,100

Statehood Date
December 14, 1819

State Number
22nd

Motto
We Dare Defend Our Rights

Song
"Alabama"

Bird
Yellowhammer

Flower
Camellia

Tree
Southern Pine

Related State Facts & Trivia

Peculiar Law
It used to be illegal to wear a false moustache in church if it made people laugh.

The reason Alabama is called the "Heart of Dixie" originally had nothing to do with Alabama! Before the Civil War (1861–1865), the Citizens Bank of Louisiana issued $10 notes that bore the French word "dix" meaning 10. This led to the South becoming known as Dixieland, and since Alabama served as the capital of the Confederacy during the Civil War, it became known as the Heart of Dixie.

Historically, Alabama's largest source of income was the cotton industry. However, in the 1930s, the boll weevil insect caused an enormous amount of damage. This, combined with competition from Texas and California, caused a significant decline in the industry. Enterprise, Alabama, is home to the first statue ever erected in honor of an insect pest, Boll Weevil Monument.

Literature

Follow the Drinking Gourd
by Jeanette Winter
(Econo-Clad Books)

This is an Underground Railroad book, in which directions to the secret path to the North were hidden in the lyrics of a song. Slaves in the fields sang the song as a way to pass information to the slaves who were getting ready to travel on the railroad to freedom. One of the clues found in the song is the reference to a river that ends between two hills. This river is the Tombigbee River, located in Alabama. ◎≈ **Cultural**

The Forty-Acre Swindle
by Dave and Neta Jackson
(Bethany House)

When his father tries to save the family farm in Alabama in 1898 by following the advice of George Washington Carver, 14-year-old Jesse struggles to help in his own way. ◎≈ **Historical Fiction**

I Am Rosa Parks
by Rosa Parks, et al.
(Dial Books)

This is a simplified version of Rosa Parks' autobiography. Her acts of civil disobedience led to the 1956 Supreme Court order to desegregate buses in Montgomery, Alabama. ◎≈ **Biography**

**If A Bus Could Talk:
The Story of Rosa Parks**
by Faith Ringgold
(Simon & Schuster)

This book tells the story of Rosa Parks in a very unique manner. It tells her life story, emphasizing the important role she played in the civil rights movement, through the voice of a talking bus. ◎≈ **Historical Fiction**

**A Picture Book
of Helen Keller**
by David A. Adler
(Holiday House)

This book features a short version of the life of Helen Keller, beginning with her birth in Alabama and focusing on her years with her beloved teacher, Annie Sullivan. ◎≈ **Biography**

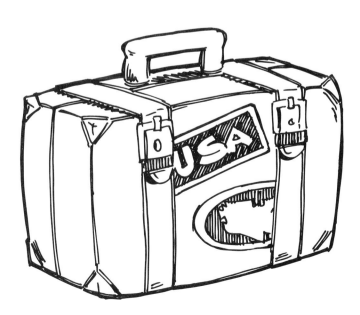

Alaska

State Flag

Wish You Were Here!

Capital
Juneau

Population
626,932

Statehood Date
January 3, 1959

State Number
49th

Motto
North to the Future

Song
"Alaska's Flag"

Bird
Willow Ptarmigan

Flower
Forget-Me-Not

Tree
Sitka Spruce

USA

Related State Facts & Trivia

Russians settled the area in the 1700s. They traded furs and made New Archangel (now known as Sitka) Alaska's first capital. Russian Orthodox churches, with their distinctive onion-shaped dome, serve as a present-day reminder of those days.

Peculiar Law
It is illegal to push a live moose out of a moving airplane.

The state flag was designed by a 13-year-old student from Chignik, Alaska. The design was chosen from 142 entries and was adopted as the territorial flag in 1927. The blue field is for the sky and the forget-me-not, the state flower. The North Star is for the future of the state of Alaska, the most northerly of the Union. The dipper is for the Great Bear—symbolizing strength.

One-fifth the size of the United States, Alaska has an area of 586,412 mi^2 (943,700 km^2) and measures 2,400 mi (3,862 km) east to west and 1,420 mi (2,285 km) north to south. This makes it larger than Texas and the next three largest states combined. In fact, if Alaska were cut into two states, each state would still be larger than Texas.

Literature

Akiak: A Tale from the Iditarod
by Robert J. Blake
(Philomel)

This is a touching, uplifting story about a sled dog (considered by many too old to participate in the Iditarod) who saves the day for her sled team and faithful owner. A map of the Iditarod routes and a day-by-day format add to this story. ◎≈ **Geography/Current Events**

Alaska's Three Bears
by Shelley Gill
(Paws IV Publishing)

Beautifully illustrated and full of information, this book tells the story of three bears: the polar bear, the grizzly bear, and the small black bear. The book has a very unique format, weaving an interesting tale of how the three bears have been driven from their original habitats and how the only place all three can be found is in Alaska. In small print, at the bottom of each page, are pertinent facts about each bear. ◎≈ **Science**

Circle of Thanks
by Susi Gregg Fowler
(Scholastic)

This is a story about how a young boy and his mother interact with the tundra animals of Alaska. This interaction begins with the rescue of a small otter pup and ends with the rescue of the boy. The characters—Otter Pup, Raven, Caribou Calf, and Arctic Fox—all participate in a "circle" of events, helping one another. ◎≈ **Science**

Dance on a Sealskin
by Barbara Winslow
(Alaska Northwest Books)

Ancient Eskimo tribal traditions, still practiced today, are detailed in this delightful story of a young Eskimo girl coming of age. The ceremonial "first dance" she must perform is done at a public gathering and initiates her as an official member of the community. This book was written and illustrated by two ladies who share their experiences of living in the Yupik villages along the Yukon River and Bering Sea in Alaska. ◎≈ **Cultural**

Danger, The Dog Yard Cat
by Libby Riddles
(Paws IV Publishing)

The story of the first woman to win the Iditarod Sled Dog Race from Anchorage to Nome, Alaska, is told in delightful verse. The central character is her cat, Danger, who lived with her and 57 sled dogs. The book includes actual photos of the dogs and cat.
◎≈ **Historical Fiction**

Thunderfeet, Alaska's Dinosaurs and Other Prehistoric Critters
by Shelley Gill
(Paws IV Publishing)

Yes, dinosaurs tread the tundra in Alaska! The story text is written in verse, in large print, on the left side of each two-page spread. On the right, in smaller print, is informational text. This book includes a useful glossary of terms. The colorful and bold illustrations highlight prehistoric animals, volcanoes, and Alaska's beautiful landscape.
◎≈ **Science/Historical Events**

Arizona

State Flag

Wish You Were Here!

Capital
Phoenix

Population
5,130,632

Statehood Date
February 14, 1912

State Number
48th

Motto
God Enriches

USA

Song
"Arizona"

Bird
Cactus Wren

Flower
Saguaro Cactus Blossom

Tree
Palo Verde

Related State Facts & Trivia

Peculiar Law
It was illegal to kick a mule. But if a mule kicked a person, it could not be prosecuted.

Arizona is full of beautiful natural attractions like the Grand Canyon and the Petrified Forest. Arizona is also home to the old London Bridge, brought over from London and reconstructed in Lake Havasu City.

Arizona has the largest Native American population of any state. More than 14 tribes are represented on 20 reservations, including part of the Navajo Nation, which is located in the Four Corners region of Arizona, Colorado, New Mexico, and Utah.

Arizona accounts for over 75% of the output of copper in the United States. The largest mine in the state is over 1,300 ft (396.2 m) deep. Copper is used in wires, cables, boilers, and radiators, but the open-pit mining does damage to the land.

Literature

Grand Canyon, Exploring a Natural Wonder
by Wendell Minor
(Scholastic)

The phenomenal beauty of the Grand Canyon is captured both in text and breathtaking watercolor illustrations by the artist/author. The author records and paints what he sees, including animal life, plant life, and geological changes on visits to the Grand Canyon throughout the seasons. ◎≋ **Geography**

Lost
by Paul Brett Johnson
and Celeste Lewis
(Orchard Books)

Based on a true story, this is an engaging saga of a little beagle lost in the Arizona desert. It is a multipurpose book because it gives a great deal of information about the desert while it weaves a tale about the love a little girl has for her lost pet and the faith she has that he will be found. ◎≋ **Geography**

A Rainbow at Night: The World in Words and Pictures
by Bruce Hucko
(Chronicle Books)

This book is a look at childhood through the drawings and paintings of 22 Navajo students, ages six to thirteen. It includes a photo of each student, a poem or description of the art in the student's own words, and other background information, including questions designed to prompt students to create their own art. ◎≋ **Cultural**

Sandra Day O'Connor: Lawyer and Supreme Court Justice
by Jean Kinney Williams
(Ferguson Publishing)

This book details Justice O'Connor's life and career, in addition to giving some background information on how a Supreme Court judge is confirmed. ◎≋ **Current Events/Biography**

Storm on the Desert
by Carolyn Lesser
(Harcourt)

The use of descriptive language enhances the beauty of this book, which shares with the reader how desert animals respond to the desert's frequent and sudden storms. The book is beautifully illustrated by Ted Rand in his easily recognizable style. ◎≋ **Geography**

Welcome to the Sea of Sand
by Jane Yolen
(Philomel)

This book features desert plants and animals and beautifully written text in verse. The author makes great use of color words and provides a detailed description of animal habits. ◎≋ **Science**

Wyatt Earp
by John F. Wukovits
(Chelsea House Publishing)

This is a biography of the gunslinger who participated in the O.K. Corral shootout near Tombstone, Arizona. ◎≋ **Biography**

Arkansas

State Flag

Wish You Were Here!

Capital
Little Rock

Population
2,673,400

Statehood Date
June 15, 1836

State Number
25th

Motto
The People Rule

Song
"Arkansas"

Bird
Mockingbird

Flower
Apple Blossom

Tree
Ponderosa Pine

Related State Facts & Trivia

Peculiar Law
It was illegal to blindfold cows on public highways.

Reptiles thrive in the warm Arkansas wilderness. Lizards, snakes, pheasants, quail, wild turkey, fox, deer, and bobcats all thrive there, too.

President Bill Clinton was born in Hope, but he grew up in Hot Springs, site of Arkansas' most popular national park.

Over 60,000 diamonds have been found by visitors to Crater of Diamonds State Park. The only active diamond mine in the United States is located near Murfreesboro. Diamonds are also Arkansas' state gem.

Little Rock got its name from a natural stone land-mark on the bank of the Arkansas River. There was also a "Big Rock" located further upstream.

Literature

Buckaroo
by Betty Traylor
(Delacorte Press Books)

When eleven-year-old Preston moves to Cotton Patch, Arkansas, in 1958, he deals with the death of his mother, the reality of segregation, and the meaning of friendship. The author makes use of 1950s vernacular (including the terms colored and nigger). Although historically accurate, such language seems insensitive by today's standards. It is especially important to host a discussion about the language prior to having students read the book. Mature students will make best use of this book. ◎≋ **General Fiction**

Days of Courage: The Little Rock Story
by Richard Kelso
(Raintree/Steck-Vaughn)

This is the story of Elizabeth Eckford, one the nine African American students who integrated Central High School in Little Rock, Arkansas, in 1957. ◎≋ **Biography/Historical Nonfiction**

Fiddlin' Sam
by Marianna Dengler
(Rising Moon)

Wandering through the Ozarks and bringing joy to people with his music, Fiddlin' Sam seeks the right person to take up his fiddle and carry on the practice. ◎≋ **Legends**

Possum Come a-Knockin'
by Nancy Van Laan
(Econo-Clad Books)

Written in a rhyme that is very inviting to students, *Possum Come a-Knockin'* is one of those "fun with language" books! There is no specific state mentioned as the setting, but the book has an Ozark Mountain feel to it. ◎≋ **General Fiction**

There Goes Lowell's Party
by Esther Hershenhorn
(Holiday House)

Lowell refuses to believe that a brewing storm will keep his resourceful Ozark relatives from celebrating his birthday. ◎≋ **General Fiction**

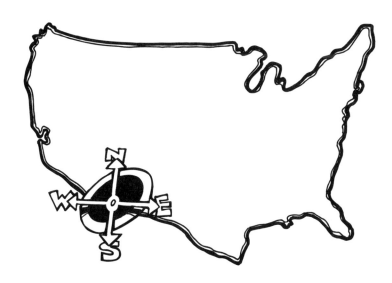

California

State Flag

CALIFORNIA REPUBLIC

Wish You Were Here!

Capital
Sacramento

Population
33,871,648

Statehood Date
September 9, 1850

State Number
31st

Motto
Eureka! (I have found it!)

USA

Song
"I Love You, California"

Bird
California Quail

Flower
Golden Poppy

Tree
California Redwood

Related State Facts & Trivia

Peculiar Law
A law created in 1925 makes it illegal to wiggle while dancing.

More people live in California than in any other state, and more immigrants settle in California than in any other state.

The highest and lowest places in the contiguous United States are both in California. Death Valley is the lowest point. It is 282 ft (85.95 m) below sea level. Mt. Whitney is the highest point at 14,491 ft (4,417 m) above sea level.

The Golden Gate Bridge connects San Francisco to the southernmost part of Marin County, California. It was completed in 1932 and is the second-longest suspension bridge in the country.

California became a major U.S. attraction long before Hollywood or Disneyland existed, when gold was discovered at Sutter's Mill on January 24, 1848. This began the Gold Rush, which brought people from all over the U.S. hoping to make their fortune in gold.

Literature

The Bracelet
by Yoshiko Uchida
(Paperstar)

In 1942, soon after the outbreak of World War II, 120,000 West Coast Japanese American citizens were forced from their homes and imprisoned in internment camps. This book tells the story of one little girl who lives in Berkeley, California. ◎≋ **Historical Fiction**

A Child's California
by Dan Harder
(Westwinds Press)

The author takes the reader on a tour of California that points out the versatility of the state. Color photographs reveal the beautiful sights and people of California. ◎≋ **Information**

City of Angels
by Julie Jaskol and
Brian Lewis
(Dutton)

Readers can take a tour of Los Angeles and visit all of the hot tourist spots. They "travel" to Farmers Market, Beverly Hills, Hollywood, Olvera Street, Griffith Park, Santa Monica, Venice Beach, and many other famous places. ◎≋ **Information**

A Day's Work
by Eve Bunting
(Clarion Books)

This is a touching story of a Mexican American boy and his grandfather who has been in the U.S. for only three days. The grandfather speaks no English and relies on the little boy to make the deal for a day's work. In the boy's eagerness to find work for them, he embellishes his grandfather's skills. ◎≋ **Current Events/General Fiction**

Gold Fever: Tales from the California Gold Rush
by Rosalyn Schanzer
(National Geographic Society)

Not just another Gold Rush book, this one was put together using actual quotes from the journals and diaries of prospectors who joined the race for gold. It is enhanced by quotes from newspaper articles written during the Gold Rush days.
◎≋ **Historical Nonfiction**

Humphrey, the Lost Whale
by Wendy Tokuda
(Econo-Clad Books)

The people of California held their collective breath for 26 days in 1985, after a humpback whale separated itself from its pod and ended up in a very small stream miles away from San Francisco Bay. The whale's miraculous rescue was made possible through the perseverance of the Californians who wouldn't give up on it. ◎≋ **Current Events**

The Rainbow Bridge
by Audrey Wood
(Harcourt)

Based on a Chumash Indian legend, this book tells the story of a magical bridge that saved an Indian tribe and brought forth dolphins. The Chumash Indians live on the coast of California. ◎≋ **Legends**

Colorado

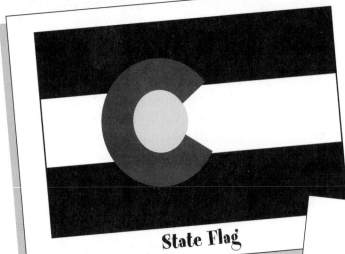

State Flag

sh You
Were Here!

Capital
Denver

Population
4,301,261

Statehood Date
August 1, 1876

State Number
38th

Motto
Nothing without
Providence

Song
"Where the Columbines Grow"

Bird
Lark Bunting

Flower
Rocky Mountain Columbine

Tree
Blue Spruce

Related State Facts & Trivia

Peculiar Law

A pet cat, if loose, must have a taillight.

Colorado has the highest average elevation of any state. More than 1,000 of its Rocky Mountain peaks reach over 10,000 ft (3,048 m) high, and 54 tower above 14,000 ft (4,267 m).

About half of Colorado is grazing land, and cattle and sheep ranching are primary industries. Corn, wheat, hay, and sugar beets are the main crops grown in Colorado. However, the state is now famous for its many ski resorts, where tourists spend 1.8 billion dollars every year.

In 1863, the first telegraph line in Colorado linked Denver with the eastern U.S. A ten-word telegram from Denver to New York City cost $9.10.

Literature

The Legend of the Whistle Pig Wrangler
by Kate Allen
(Kumquat Press)

This cowboy tale is set in the southwestern part of Colorado. The illustrator has hidden a hummingbird on each page, adding some fun to reading this book. An added highlight is a glossary of cowboy terms at the back of the book. ◎≋ **General Fiction**

Mountain Town
by Bonnie and Arthur Geisert
(Houghton Mifflin)

The authors take the reader on a leisurely trip through the mountain villages of Colorado. ◎≋ **Geography**

A Personal Tour of Mesa Verde
by Robert Young
(Lerner Publications Company)

This book presents a tour of the Anasazi cliff dwellings in Colorado through the eyes of some of the people who lived and visited there nearly 800 years ago. ◎≋ **Historical Fiction**

Silver Dollar Girl
by Katherine Ayres
(Delacorte Press Books)

In 1885, unhappy living with her aunt and uncle in Pittsburgh, Valentine Harper disguises herself as a boy and runs away to Colorado. She is determined to find her father who has gone there in search of gold. ◎≋ **Historical Fiction**

Connecticut

State Flag

Capital
Hartford

Population
3,405,565

Statehood Date
January 9, 1788

State Number
5th

Motto
He Who Transplanted
Still Sustains

Song
"Yankee Doodle"

Bird
Robin

Flower
Mountain Laurel

Tree
White Oak

USA

Related State Facts & Trivia

Peculiar Law
Building a dam used to be forbidden unless you were a beaver.

The world's first written constitution, the Fundamental Orders, was created in 1639 by English settlements that united to form the Connecticut Colony. That's why Connecticut is often referred to as the Constitution State.

Connecticut is home to the oldest U.S. newspaper still being published: *The Hartford Courant*, established in 1764.

Most of Connecticut's income is from industry and commerce, but the state is still known for its small farms. Corn is the chief vegetable grown in the state.

Connecticut natives were very patriotic during the Revolutionary War (1775–1783). About half of George Washington's troops in New York in 1776 were from Connecticut.

Literature

Autumn Moon: Seasons of the Moon (Vol. 1.)
by Jean Craighead George
(HarperTrophy)

The author describes how a young buck endures the devastation following a hurricane in the salt marshes along the Connecticut coast. ◎≋ **Science**

The Courage of Sarah Noble
by Alice Dalgliesh
(Atheneum Books)

This is the story of eight-year-old Sarah, who courageously accompanies her father into the Connecticut wilderness of the 1700s and then stays with an Indian family in her father's absence. ◎≋ **Historical Fiction**

Here We All Are
by Tomie dePaola
(Puffin)

This is the second in a series about the childhood of author and illustrator Tomie dePaola, who grew up in Connecticut. ◎≋ **Autobiography**

Redcoats and Petticoats
by Katherine Kirkpatrick
(Holiday House)

This is the story of the Setauket Spy Ring that was in operation during the Revolutionary War. Brave men, women, and children carried information from the British-occupied Long Island to the Patriot-held Fairfield, Connecticut. ◎≋ **Historical Fiction**

Through the Lock
by Carol Otis Hurst
(Houghton Mifflin)

Etta, a twelve-year-old orphan in nineteenth-century Connecticut, meets a boy living in an abandoned cabin on the New Haven and Northampton Canal and has adventures with him while trying to reunite with her siblings. ◎≋ **Historical Fiction**

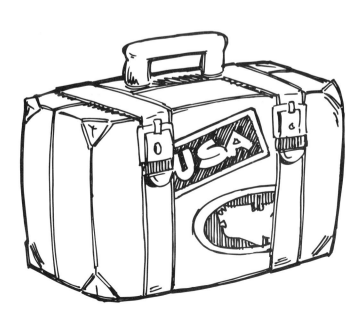

Delaware

DECEMBER 7, 1787

State Flag

Wish You Were Here!

Capital
Dover

Population
783,600

Statehood Date
December 7, 1787

State Number
1st

Motto
Liberty and Independence

Song
"Our Delaware"

Bird
Blue Hen Chicken

Flower
Peach Blossom

Tree
American Holly

Related State Facts & Trivia

Peculiar Law
It is illegal to fly over any body of water, unless one is carrying sufficient supplies of food and drink.

England gave Delaware to William Penn, founder of Pennsylvania, in 1682 to be part of Pennsylvania. But in the Revolutionary War, Delaware fought as a separate state. The state's nickname is the "First State" because it was the first state to ratify the U.S. Constitution in 1787.

Delaware has good soil for farming and is well-known for its fishing. The state's main crops are soybeans, corn, potatoes, and mushrooms. The primary commercial fish is the Menhaden (a type of herring), but sport fishermen also find bass, carp, catfish, eels, pike, trout, and white perch.

The ladybug was adopted as the official state insect in 1974 after a group of elementary school students convinced the state legislature to do so.

Literature

And Still the Turtle Watched
by Sheila MacGill-Callahan
(Econo-Clad Books)

This book tells the story of how many years ago, a Delaware Indian and his grandson stood on a cliff overlooking a valley. The grandfather showed the boy where he would carve a turtle's head and explained that it would remain there throughout the years to watch over the Delaware people. ◎≋ **Legend**

Come Morning
by Leslie Davis Guccione
(Carolrhoda Books)

Twelve-year-old Freedom, the son of a freed slave living in Delaware in the early 1850s, takes over his father's work in the Underground Railroad when his father disappears. ◎≋ **Historical Fiction**

Crossing the Delaware:
A History in Many Voices
by Louise Peacock
(Atheneum Books)

The author presents the events leading up to the Battle of Trenton, the battle itself, and its aftermath, as told through historical excerpts, a tour of Washington's crossing, and a series of fictionalized letters. ◎≋ **Historical Fiction**

The Lenape Indians
by Josh Wilker
(Chelsea House)

This book examines the history, culture, and future prospects of the Lenape (also known as Delaware) Indians. ◎≋ **Information**

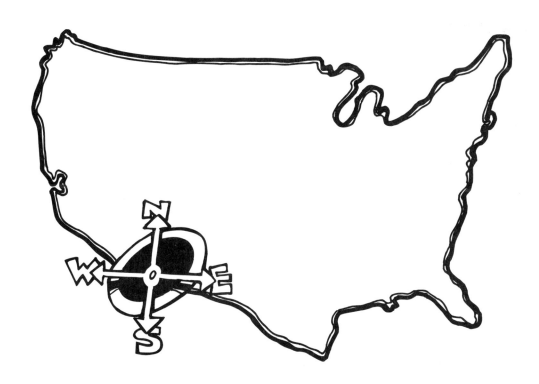

Florida

State Flag

Wish You Were Here!

Capital
Tallahassee

Population
15,982,378

Statehood Date
March 3, 1845

State Number
27th

Motto
In God We Trust

Song
"Swanee River"

Bird
Mockingbird

Flower
Orange Blossom

Tree
Sabal Palmetto Pine

USA

Related State Facts & Trivia

Peculiar Law
It is against the law to put live-stock on a school bus.

Pelican Island was the first federal wildlife refuge in the U.S. It was established by President Theodore Roosevelt in 1903.

The John F. Kennedy Space Center in Cape Canaveral is the site for space shuttle launches. It was also from here that the lunar-landing flight carrying Neil Armstrong, the first man on the moon, took off.

Alligators still live in the wild subtropical swamplands of Florida. They grow up to 19 ft (5.8 m) long. They eat fish, frogs, snakes, and small mammals such as deer.

More passenger ships pass through Miami's port than any other city in the U.S.

Literature

Everglades
by Jean Craighead George
(HarperTrophy)

Breathtaking paintings by Wendell Minor are an added feature to this environmental tale set in the Florida Everglades. The story is told through the dialogue of an Indian guide and a group of school students in a boat that he paddles through the Everglades. The book presents the problems facing unique ecosystems in today's growing world. ◎≋ **Science**

A Guatemalan Family
by Michael Malone
(Lerner Publications Company)

This book describes a Guatemalan family's struggle to emigrate from their country to the United States and the adjustments they make. ◎≋ **Cultural**

Jumping off to Freedom
by Anilú Bernardo
(Econo-Clad Books)

Courage and desperation lead 15-year-old David and his father to flee Cuba's repressive regime and seek freedom by taking to the sea on a raft headed for Miami. ◎≋ **Cultural/Current Events**

A Land Remembered
by Patrick D. Smith
(Pineapple Press)

A Florida family battles the hardships of the frontier to rise from a poor life to the wealth and standing of real estate tycoons. The sweeping story begins in 1858 and ends in 1968 and is rich in Florida history. ◎≋ **Historical Fiction**

Manatee Morning
by Jim Arnosky
(Simon & Schuster)

A mother manatee and her baby swim in the warm waters of the Crystal River in Florida. The book is written in verse. ◎≋ **Science**

Panther, Shadow of the Swamp
by Jonathan London
(Candlewick Press)

The reader is treated to a day in the life of a panther as a mother cat slinks through the Florida Everglades hunting for food. She has a special mission: a litter of hungry kittens await her return. As an added feature, the author has included an information page at the end of the book that tells about the dwindling number of panthers in America today. ◎≋ **Geography/Science**

The Young Naturalist's Guide to Florida
by Peggy Sias Lantz and Wendy A. Hale
(Pineapple Press)

This book covers a wide spectrum of topics: from Florida's weather patterns to its habitats to its endangered species. It also covers each of Florida's geographic regions separately and provides some interesting history. ◎≋ **Science**

Georgia

State Flag

Wish You Were Here!

Capital
Atlanta

Population
8,186,453

Statehood Date
January 2, 1788

State Number
4th

Motto
Wisdom, Justice,
and Moderation

Song
"Georgia on My Mind"

Bird
Brown Thrasher

Flower
Cherokee Rose

Tree
Live Oak

Related State Facts & Trivia

Peculiar Law
No one may carry an ice-cream cone in his or her back pocket on Sundays.

Coca-Cola was developed in Atlanta by a pharmacist named John Pemberton.

The Girl Scouts of the U.S.A. was founded in Georgia by Juliette Gordon Low in 1912.

Forests once extended over the whole state. Today, 70% of Georgia is covered with trees. The state ranks first in the growth of timber. Pine trees yield pulpwood, which is used to make paper.

The Cherokee Phoenix was the first known newspaper to be printed in a Native American language. It was published in New Echota in 1828.

Literature

Christmas in Georgia
by Celestine Sibley
(Peachtree Publishers)

This is a collection of Christmastime tales set in Georgia.
◎≈ **General Fiction**

The Forgotten Tunnel:
A Savannah Mystery
by Nancie M. Clark
(Shapiro Publishing)

This chapter book features the history and landmarks of Savannah, Georgia, the colony's first city. Brad Pierce moves to Savannah and faces his fears of the city's ghostly past and his spooky home.
◎≈ **Historical Fiction (Mystery)**

Now Let Me Fly
by Dolores Johnson
(Aladdin)

This is the story of a slave family, from the capture of a young girl in Africa to her life on a plantation in Georgia. The author gives a vivid depiction of the hardships on the slave ship and the unhappy lives the slaves endured. Although the characters are pure fiction, the author has compiled accounts of actual slave families, giving the book a sense of historical authenticity. ◎≈ **Historical Fiction**

Pink and Say
by Patricia Polacco
(Philomel)

Passed down through the years, starting with the author's great-great-grandfather, *Pink and Say* is not just another Civil War story. Beginning in a pasture in Georgia and ending at Andersonville Prison, the book tells the story of two young Union soldiers, one black and one white, and the deep bond between them. The love and respect they share for Abraham Lincoln is an important element of the story. ◎≈ **Historical Fiction**

Sky Sash So Blue
by Libby Hathorn
(Simon & Schuster)

This touching tale, written in verse, describes the efforts of the mother of a slave family to make a real wedding day for her daughter. The special day includes a treasured blue sash, which will be used for future weddings in the family. ◎≈ **General Fiction**

Hawaii

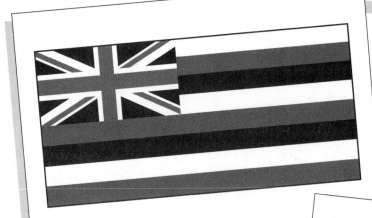

State Flag

Capital
Honolulu

Population
1,211,537

Statehood Date
August 21, 1959

State Number
50th

Motto
The Life of the Land is Perpetuated in Righteousness

Song
"Hawaii Ponoi" (Hawaii's Own)

Bird
Nene (Hawaiian Goose)

Flower
Yellow Hibiscus

Tree
Kukui (Candlenut Tree)

Related State Facts & Trivia

Peculiar Law
It used to be illegal to insert pennies in one's ears.

The Hawaiian alphabet has only 12 letters: a, e, h, i, k, l, m, n, o, p, u, w.

The wettest place on earth is Mount Waialeale on Kauai. It receives an average of 460 inches (11.60 m) of rain a year.

Pineapples are not native to Hawaii, although they have become an important state crop. The state is the world's biggest exporter of the fruit. Sugar cane, however, is the main export.

Hawaii was originally ruled by Polynesian monarchs before it became a republic in 1894.

Literature

Dumpling Soup
by Jama Kim Rattigan
(Little, Brown and Company)

Rich in Hawaiian tradition, this book tells the story of a little girl who gets her first chance to make dumplings for the large New Year's celebration her family enjoys every year. This book includes English, Hawaiian, Japanese, and Korean glossaries and the recipe for Dumpling Soup. ◎≋ **Cultural**

The Island-below-the-Star
by James Rumford
(Houghton Mifflin)

This book is beautifully written and illustrated. It tells the story of the discovery of the Hawaiian Islands by an adventuresome group of brothers. ◎≋ **Historical Fiction**

Luka's Quilt
by Georgia Guback
(Greenwillow Books)

This is the story of a little girl and her grandmother. Her grandmother is making her a traditional Hawaiian quilt, and the little girl is very excited about it . . . until it is finished. ◎≋ **Cultural**

Punia and the King of Sharks
by Lee Wardlaw
(Dial Books)

An adaptation of an old Hawaiian folktale, this book tells the story of a young boy who is trying to trick the king of the sharks who killed his father. The boy succeeds but nearly loses his own life in his quest. There is a handy glossary and pronunciation guide of Hawaiian terms at the beginning of the book. ◎≋ **Legends**

Remember Pearl Harbor: American and Japanese Survivors Tell Their Stories
by Thomas B. Allen
(National Geographic Society)

Photographs and maps help make this an effective narrative built from first-person oral histories. Both sides of this story are humanized and fairly presented in a sound, historical context.
◎≋ **Historical Nonfiction**

Idaho

State Flag

Wish You Were Here!

Capital
Boise

Population
1,293,953

Statehood Date
July 3, 1890

State Number
43rd

Motto
It is Forever

Song
"Here We Have Idaho"

Bird
Mountain Bluebird

Flower
Syringa

Tree
Western White Pine

Related State Facts & Trivia

Peculiar Law
It was illegal to fish for trout from the back of a giraffe.

The longest main street in the U.S. is in Island Park. It runs for 33 mi (53.11 km).

Idaho was the last of the 50 states to be sighted. It was "discovered" when Lewis and Clark passed through the region with Sacagawea in 1805.

Gold can be found in some form in every county in Idaho. The state also produces 72 different kinds of gemstones, some of which can not be found anywhere else in the world. Idaho was the leading silver producer in the United States until the falling price of silver forced many mines to close. There are still many gold and silver ghost towns in Idaho.

Literature

Baseball Saved Us
by Ken Mochizuki
(Lee & Low Books)

During World War II, the author's parents were sent to the Minidoka Japanese internment camp in Idaho. He has written a story about a young boy whose father decides to build a baseball field and start a camp league. Baseball helped to occupy their thoughts and curb the bitterness that was growing in their hearts. This story addresses a difficult time in our nation's history. ◎≈ **Cultural/Historical Fiction**

Destination: Rocky Mountains
by Jonathan Grupper
(National Geographic Society)

Full-color photographs of wildlife and scenery fill the pages of this book. By carefully combining the illustrations and the text, the author conveys a real feeling for the vastness, variety, and richness of the Rocky Mountains. ◎≈ **Geography**

The Garden of Eden Motel
by Morse Hamilton
(Greenwillow Books)

In the early 1950s, eleven-year-old Dal accompanies his stepfather, Mr. Sabatini, on a business trip to a rural community in Idaho. Dal makes new friends and becomes involved in a scheme involving a uranium mine. ◎≈ **Historical Fiction**

Mailing May
by Michael O. Tunnell
(Greenwillow Books)

In 1914, there wasn't money enough to buy a train ticket for little May to make the long-awaited trip across the Idaho mountains to visit her grandma. Through the ingenuity of her parents, her willing spirit, and the help of the U.S. Postal Service, May gets to make the trip. The story is based on an actual event. ◎≈ **Historical Fiction**

Mountain Town
by Bonnie Geisert
(Houghton Mifflin)

This book describes a year in the present-day life of a mountain town that was founded when prospectors searching for gold arrived in the Rocky Mountains in the mid-nineteenth century. ◎≈ **Geography/Historical Nonfiction**

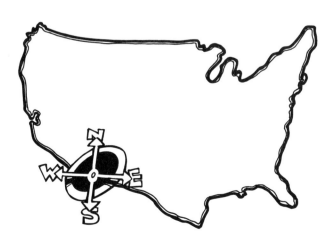

Illinois

State Flag

Wish You Were Here!

Capital
Springfield

Population
12,419,293

Statehood Date
December 3, 1818

State Number
21st

Motto
State Sovereignty—
National Union

Song
"Illinois"

Bird
Cardinal

Flower
Native Violet

Tree
White Oak

Related State Facts & Trivia

Peculiar Law
Catching fish with dynamite used to be forbidden.

Kaskaskia Island is the only part of Illinois that is west of the Mississippi River.

More soybeans are grown in Illinois that in any other state. The town of Decatur has the label "soybean capital of the world." The soybean is also the second most important crop, after corn, in the U.S.

The Home Insurance Building in Chicago was the first metal-frame skyscraper in the world. It was built in 1884 and rose ten stories high. Chicago is the third largest city in the U.S.

Literature

Abe Lincoln Goes to Washington
by Cheryl Harness
(National Geographic Society)

The first half of this book depicts Lincoln's life in Springfield, Illinois, where he met and married Mary Todd and became more and more well-known. His political aspirations began to blossom during this time. The second half of the book deals with his rise to the presidency, his move to Washington, D.C., and his assassination. ◎≋ **Biography**

Casey Jones
by Allan Drummond
(Farrar, Straus & Giroux)

This is the true story of John Luther Jones, better known as Casey Jones. It is written in high-spirited verse and tells the story of his famous trip on the Illinois 638. ◎≋ **Historical Nonfiction**

Hog Music
by Mary-Claire Helldorfer
(Viking)

Hog Music tells the story of a little girl who is moving with her family to Illinois. She is sad to say good-bye to her grandmother and tries to convince her to come with them. Her grandmother's reply is that there is nothing but "hog music" in Illinois. Her grandmother sends her a birthday present that has an adventure of its own.
◎≋ **Historical Fiction**

The Journey
by Sarah Stewart
(Farrar, Straus & Giroux)

Hannah is a young Amish girl who gets to take a once-in-a-lifetime trip to Chicago. She shares her adventures through her diary, which she calls her "silent friend." Although the city holds many new sights, each one of them reminds her, in one way or another, of home.
◎≋ **Cultural/Geography**

Mr. Lincoln's Whiskers
by Karen B. Winnick
(Boyds Mills Press)

Eleven-year-old Grace Bedell sent a letter to Abraham Lincoln in Springfield, Illinois, just prior to the presidential election, telling him that he would look better if he wore a beard. This book features a copy of her letter to Abraham Lincoln and his reply. ◎≋ **Biography**

Indiana

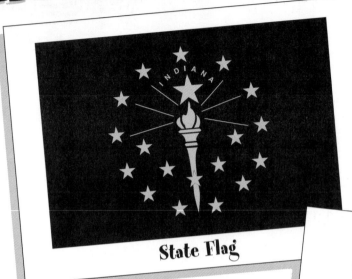

State Flag

Wish You Were Here!

Capital
Indianapolis

Population
6,080,485

Statehood Date
December 11, 1816

State Number
19th

Motto
Crossroads of America

Song
"On the Banks of the Wabash, Far Away"

Bird
Cardinal

Flower
Peony

Tree
Tulip-Poplar

Related State Facts & Trivia

Peculiar Law: Taking a bath during the wintertime was forbidden.

Woodchucks, a member of the squirrel family, are common in Indiana. They are also known as groundhogs.

Every year, the Indianapolis 500 auto race is begun with the words, "Gentlemen, start your engines."

Indianapolis has more major highways than any other city in the United States.

Born in Indiana, William Henry Harrison was the 9th president, but his term of office lasted barely one month in 1841. While delivering the inaugural address, he caught a cold, which turned into a fatal case of pneumonia. He was the first president to die in office.

Literature

The Floating House
by Scott Russell Sanders
(Atheneum Books)

In 1815, the McClures sail their flatboat from Pittsburgh down the Ohio River and settle in what would later become Indiana.
◎≋ **Historical Fiction**

Indiana Days: Life in a Frontier Town
by Catherine E. Chambers
(Troll)

In the 1840s twelve-year-old Kristi travels from her family's sod house on the Iowa prairie to an Indiana town to stay with relatives and get an education. ◎≋ **Historical Fiction**

A Place Called Freedom
by Scott Russell Sanders
(Atheneum Books)

Based on the founding of Lyle Station, Indiana, this book shares a touching story of how freed and runaway slaves made their way to Indiana and settled there. ◎≋ **Historical Fiction**

President of the Underground Railroad: A Story About Levi Coffin
by Gwenyth Swain
(Carolrhoda Books)

This biography tells the story of a Quaker man from North Carolina whose fearless work on the Underground Railroad in Indiana and Ohio helped thousands of men and women escape the cruelty of slavery. ◎≋ **Biography**

Ruthie's Gift
by Kimberly Brubaker Bradley
(Doubleday Books)

Just before the beginning of World War I, eight-year-old Ruthie, who lives with her parents and six brothers on a farm in Indiana, wishes for a sister and tries to behave like the lady her mother wants her to be. ◎≋ **Historical Fiction**

Turn Homeward, Hannalee
by Patricia Beatty
(William Morrow & Company)

Twelve-year-old Hannalee Reed, forced to relocate in Indiana along with other Georgia mill workers during the Civil War, leaves her mother with a promise to return home as soon as the war ends.
◎≋ **Historical Fiction**

Young Abe Lincoln
by Cheryl Harness
(National Geographic Society)

Although this book begins with Abe Lincoln's birth in Kentucky and ends with his arrival in Springfield, Illinois, it centers on his childhood in Indiana. It is a beautifully illustrated book. ◎≋ **Biography**

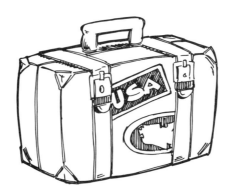

Iowa

State Flag

Wish You Were Here!

Capital
Des Moines

Population
2,926,324

Statehood Date
December 28, 1846

State Number
29th

Motto
Our Liberties We Prize and
Our Rights We Shall Maintain

Song
"The Song of Iowa"

Bird
American Goldfinch

Flower
Wild Rose

Tree
Oak

USA

Related State Facts & Trivia

Peculiar Law
It used to be illegal for a woman not to wear a corset.

Iowa produces 25% of the nation's pigs and hogs. (Hogs are pigs that weigh over 120 lbs or 50 kg.) Corn is the pig's main food, and Iowa grows that, too.

The red delicious apple (the most popular apple in the U.S.) was developed in East Peru.

The shortest and steepest railroad in the U.S. is in Dubuque. It is 296 ft (90.22 m) long, and rises at an incline of 60 degrees to a height of 189 ft (57.61 m).

Maid-Rites were invented in Muscatine, Iowa. Maid-Rites were one of the original hamburgers: a meat sandwich made of finely ground hamburger. The hamburger was cooked and put on a bun and then served with mustard, pickles, or chopped onions.

Literature

Addie's Forever Friend
by Laurie Lawlor
(Albert Whitman)

This short chapter books details a summer of changes for an eight-year-old girl in early Iowa. ◎≋ **Historical Fiction**

The Big Rivers
by Bruce Hiscock
(Atheneum Books)

This book presents an interesting and factual tale of the Mississippi, Missouri, and Ohio Rivers and the devastating floods they cause. Several states are affected each year, but this book deals primarily with Iowa. ◎≋ **Geography**

Prairie Town
by Bonnie and Arthur Geisert
(Houghton Mifflin)

The authors take the readers on a trip through middle America, visiting small cities and cornfields along the way. This book has very busy, fact-filled, and informative illustrations. ◎≋ **Geography**

Those Calculating Crows!
by Ali P. Wakefield
(Simon & Schuster)

Based on an experiment from many years ago, crows seem to be able to count … at least up to seven. This book is funny, it presents a problem with a solution, and it has a mystery to be solved. The author doesn't state a particular setting, but Iowa seems to be a perfect spot since it is one of the country's biggest corn states. ◎≋ **Science/Current Events**

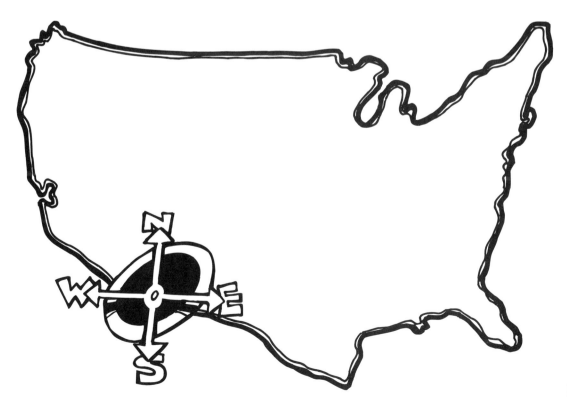

Kansas

State Flag

ish You
Were Here!

Capital
Topeka

Population
2,688,418

Statehood Date
January 29, 1861

State Number
34th

Motto
To the Stars
through Difficulties

USA

Song
"Home on the Range"

Bird
Western Meadowlark

Flower
Sunflower

Tree
Cottonwood

Related State Facts & Trivia

Peculiar Law
It is illegal to drive a buffalo through a street.

Kansas was the first state to include prohibition of alcohol in its constitution in 1880.

Amelia Earhart, the famous American pilot, was born in Kansas in 1897. She was the first woman to fly solo across the Atlantic in 1932. In 1937, she and a navigator attempted to fly around the world, but her plane was lost in the Pacific Ocean, with less than one-third of her journey remaining.

Kansas is a leading state in the manufacture of aircraft. Commercial, private, and military planes have been made here.

Literature

Aunt Minnie McGranahan
by Mary Skillings Prigger
(Clarion Books)

The townspeople in St. Clere, Kansas, are sure it will never work out when the neat and orderly spinster, Minnie McGranahan, takes her nine orphaned nieces and nephews into her home in 1920.
◎≋ **Historical Fiction**

Friends and Enemies
by Louann Bigge Gaeddert
(Atheneum Books)

In 1941 in Kansas, as America enters World War II, 14-year-old William finds himself alienated from his friend Jim, a Mennonite who does not believe in fighting for any reason, as they argue about the war.
◎≋ **Historical Fiction/Cultural**

Heat Wave
by Helen Ketteman
(Walker & Company)

A wildly funny tale, this book is about a young brother and sister who live on a farm in Kansas. The focus of the story is a horrendous heat wave that hits their town. ◎≋ **General Fiction/Tall Tales**

In the Face of Danger
by Joan Lowery Nixon
(Laurel-Leaf Books)

Deeply unhappy about her family's separation because of poverty, Megan gradually finds contentment and purpose in her new home on the Kansas prairie with a kind and loving adopted family.
◎≋ **Historical Fiction**

Jim-Dandy
by Hadley Irwin
(Troll Communications)

Living after the Civil War on a Kansas homestead with his stern stepfather, 13-year-old Caleb raises a beloved colt and becomes involved in General Custer's raids on the Cheyenne.
◎≋ **Historical Fiction**

The Monument
by Gary Paulsen
(Econo-Clad Books)

Thirteen-year-old Rocky, self-conscious about the brace on her leg, has her life changed by the remarkable artist who comes to her small Kansas town to design a war memorial. ◎≋ **Historical Fiction**

Wagon Wheels
by Barbara Brenner
(HarperTrophy)

Shortly after the Civil War, a black family travels to Kansas to take advantage of the free land offered through the Homestead Act.
◎≋ **Historical Fiction**

Kentucky

State Flag

Wish You Were Here!

Capital
Frankfort

Population
4,041,769

Statehood Date
June 1, 1792

State Number
15th

Motto
United We Stand,
Divided We Fall

Song
"My Old Kentucky Home"

Bird
Cardinal

Flower
Goldenrod

Tree
Tulip-Poplar

Related State Facts & Trivia

Peculiar Law

It is the law that a person must take a bath once a year.

Muhammad Ali (born Cassius Clay in 1942) is a native Kentuckian. He is the only boxer to win the world heavyweight title three times. He also won an Olympic gold medal in 1960.

The Shakers are a small religious group who follow a very simple way of life. They use traditional farming methods and are known world-wide for their well-made furniture. The Shaker village at Pleasant Hill was established in the 1800s.

The Kentucky Derby is the oldest continuously held horse race in the country. It is held at Churchill Downs in Louisville on the first Saturday in May. The bluegrass country around Lexington is the home of some of the world's finest race horses.

Literature

Daniel Boone
by Laurie Lawlor
(Albert Whitman)

This is a well-written biography of the famous frontiersman.
◎≈ **Biography**

Down Cut Shin Creek:
The Packhorse Librarians
of Kentucky
by Kathi Appelt
(HarperCollins)

The book opens with a chapter on President Franklin D. Roosevelt's
New Deal and WPA programs, continues with a fictionalized account
of one workday for a pack-horse librarian as she covers a 20-mile route,
and then offers some information on the formation and design of the
program. ◎≈ **Historical Nonfiction**

Leo the Magnificat
by Ann M. Martin
(Scholastic)

Leo is a stray cat that wanders into a churchyard in Louisville, Kentucky.
He becomes a member of the church family and spends the rest of
his life there, attending church regularly. This tale is based on a true
story. ◎≈ **General Fiction**

The Tin Heart
by Karen Ackerman
(Atheneum Books)

This Civil War story has an interesting twist. It deals with the friendship
between two young girls who live across the Ohio River from each
other: one is in Kentucky and one is in Ohio. These states are on oppo-
site sides when the war breaks out, and it appears their friendship
could be in trouble. ◎≈ **Historical Fiction**

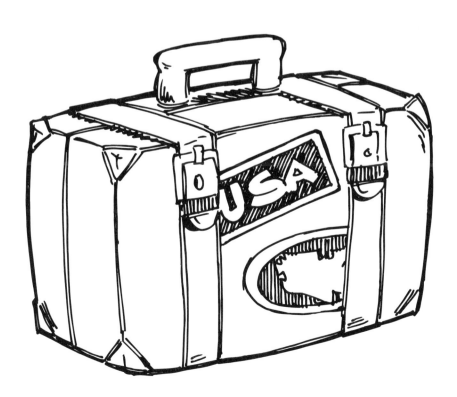

Louisiana

State Flag

UNION, JUSTICE & CONFIDENCE

Wish You Were Here!

Capital
Baton Rouge

Population
4,468,976

Statehood Date
April 30, 1812

State Number
18th

Motto
Union, Justice, and Confidence

USA

Song
"Give Me Louisiana"

Bird
Brown Pelican

Flower
Magnolia

Tree
Bald Cypress

Related State Facts & Trivia

Peculiar Law
By law, any person had the right to grow as tall as he or she liked.

The name po'boy came from the fact that the sandwich would be so stuffed with the ingredients that you could buy an extra loaf of bread and take all the ingredients that had fallen off as you ate it and make a whole extra sandwich. So poor boys could afford to feed their whole family off one sandwich.

Mardi Gras, which is French for "Fat Tuesday," is a celebration that is known worldwide. It is an ancient custom that originated in southern Europe. It celebrates food and fun just before the 40 days of Lent (a Catholic time of prayer and sacrifice). In New Orleans, this celebration includes a parade of costumed merrymakers who dance, sing, and march through the streets.

Because of its many bays and sounds, Louisiana has the longest coastline (15,000 mi or 24,140 km) of any state and 41 percent of the nation's wetlands.

Literature

Cajun Alphabet
by James Rice
(Pelican Publishing
Company)

A friendly alligator provides an interesting and practical lesson in Cajun French. This book also includes a glossary of essential Cajun words. ◎≈ **Cultural**

Keeper of the Swamp
by Ann Garrett
(Turtle Books)

Absolutely breathtaking illustrations highlight this book about a young boy coming of age in the Louisiana Bayou. He and his grandfather are on a mission to preserve and protect the swamp and its animal life. Informational pages on swamps and alligators appear at the back of the book. ◎≈ **Science**

Six Foolish Fishermen
by Robert D. San Souci
(Hyperion Press)

The author hilariously presents this cajun folktale. The story is about six cajun friends who try to spend a day fishing with one thing after another going wrong. ◎≈ **Legend**

The Story of Ruby Bridges
by Robert Coles
(Scholastic)

This is the true story of Ruby Bridges, the first black student to attend an all-white school in New Orleans, Louisiana. On November 14, 1960, Ruby walked up the steps to the front door of the school accompanied by U.S. Marshals. ◎≈ **Biography/Historical Nonfiction**

Through My Eyes
by Ruby Bridges
(Scholastic)

In her own words, Ruby Bridges recalls the events surrounding her history-making integration of an elementary school in New Orleans, Louisiana, in 1960. At six years old, she was accompanied by U.S. Marshals and spent most of the year in school alone. This brave little girl was depicted on her way to school in the now-famous Norman Rockwell illustration. ◎≈ **Autobiography/Historical Nonfiction**

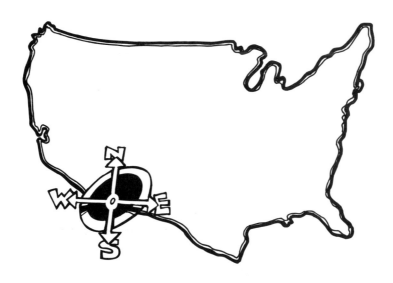

Maine

State Flag

Wish You Were Here!

Capital
Augusta

Population
1,274,923

Statehood Date
March 15, 1820

State Number
23rd

Motto
I direct

Song
"State of Maine Song"

Bird
Brown-Capped Chickadee

Flower
White Pine Cone and Tassel

Tree
White Pine

Related State Facts & Trivia

Peculiar Law
It was illegal to walk the streets with your shoelaces undone.

Maine has 62 lighthouses. One of the most famous is Portland Head Light, which was commissioned by President George Washington.

Almost 89% of Maine is forested. The abundance of timber has encouraged several arts and crafts industries, including block and silkscreen printing, furniture making, and wood carving.

Nearly 90% of the nation's lobster supply is caught off the coast of Maine, approximately 40 million lbs (18,140,000 kg). Other ocean products that come from Maine include ocean perch, herring, scallops, shrimp, sardines, and Atlantic salmon.

There is evidence that Native Americans were living in Maine more than 2,000 years ago.

Literature

The Bunyans
by Audrey Wood
(Scholastic)

This is a very tall tale about a very tall family: the Bunyans. They travel a great deal, but their home base is Maine. ◎≈ **Legend**

Calico Bush
by Rachel Field
(Simon & Schuster)

This classic pioneer story is about Marguerite, a young French orphan in the New World, who promises to serve the Sargent family for six long years in return for shelter, food and clothing. ◎≈ **Historical Fiction**

I Wonder If I'll See A Whale
by Frances Ward Weller
(Econo-Clad Books)

A young girl who has spent many an hour on whale observation boats is hoping to finally see a whale. She's seen their shadows and their far-off spouts, but she's never really seen a whale. Finally, the day arrives that she does. Her dream is realized. This book is filled with lots of information about whales. The dedication mentions a special hump-back whale the author observed in the Gulf of Maine. ◎≈ **Science**

Jigsaw Jackson
by David F. Birchman
(Lothrop, Lee & Shepard)

This original tall tale is about a farmer from Maine who discovers he is a wizard at putting together jigsaw puzzles. This book is full of exciting and farfetched accomplishments. All the excitement loses its appeal when the farmer thinks about home and how he misses it. ◎≈ **Legend**

Maryland

State Flag

Wish You Were Here!

Capital
Annapolis

Population
5,296,486

Statehood Date
April 28, 1788

State Number
7th

Motto
Manly Deeds,
Womanly Words

Song
"Maryland, My Maryland"

Bird
Baltimore Oriole

Flower
Black-Eyed Susan

Tree
White Oak

Related State Facts & Trivia

Peculiar Law
It was illegal in parts of Maryland to mistreat an oyster.

In 1649, Maryland passed a law guaranteeing religious freedom. This law was originally intended to protect the rights of new immigrants to practice Catholicism. This made Maryland the first colony to officially practice religious toleration.

Maryland was a slave state, but it never left the Union and wasn't dominated by plantations. It was the site of some of the fiercest fighting of the Civil War.

Crabs are a large part of Maryland's fishing industry. Fishing for crabs is a favorite pastime and does not require a license.

Maryland was inhabited by Indians as early as about 10,000 B.C. Permanent Indian villages were established by about A.D.1,000.

Literature

Anna on the Farm
by Mary Downing Hahn
(Clarion Books)

Nine-year-old Anna is happy to spend a week at her aunt and uncle's farm in Beltsville, Maryland, until she meets Theodore, who calls her a "city slicker" and spurs her to prove that she's just as clever and brave as he is. ◎≈ **Historical Fiction**

Assateague: Island of the Wild Ponies
by Andrea Jauck and Larry Points
(Sierra Press)

This book describes the life and natural environment of the pony breed that lives on the long barrier island off the Maryland and Virginia coast. ◎≈ **Science**

Aunt Harriet's Underground Railroad in the Sky
by Faith Ringgold
(Econo-Clad Books)

The author gives a unique presentation of Harriet Tubman's role as a conductor on the Underground Railroad, which helped slaves reach the North and freedom in the years prior to the Civil War. She led slaves to freedom via many routes, but the majority of them began near the plantation in Bucktown, Maryland, where she was born. This book contains a bibliography of Harriet Tubman, and brightly colored, collage-type illustrations add interest to the story. ◎≈ **Biography**

The Biggest (And Best) Flag That Ever Flew
by Rebecca C. Jones
(Tidewater Publishing)

The author recounts how Mrs. Pickergill of Baltimore was commissioned to make the huge flag that flew at Fort McHenry over Baltimore Harbor during a battle with the British in 1814. ◎≈ **Historical Nonfiction**

Lord Baltimore: English Politician and Colonist
by Loree Lough, et al.
(Chelsea House Publishing)

This is a biography of the Catholic baron who became the founder of the state of Maryland. ◎≈ **Biography**

Molly Bannaky
by Alice McGill
(Houghton Mifflin)

This book describes how Benjamin Banneker's grandmother journeyed from England to Maryland in the late seventeenth century, worked as an indentured servant, began a farm of her own, and married a freed slave. ◎≈ **Historical Fiction**

Retreat From Gettysburg
by Kathleen Ernst
(Burd Street Press)

In 1863, during the tense week after the Battle of Gettysburg, a Maryland boy faces difficult choices as he is forced to care for a wounded Confederate officer while trying to decide if he himself should leave his family to fight for the Union. ◎≈ **Historical Fiction**

Massachusetts

State Flag

ish You
Were Here!

Capital
Boston

Population
6,349,097

Statehood Date
February 6, 1788

State Number
6th

Motto
By the Sword We Seek Peace, but Peace Only Under Liberty

Song
"All Hail to Massachusetts"

Bird
Black-Capped Chickadee

Flower
Trailing Arbutus

Tree
American Elm

USA

Related State Facts & Trivia

Peculiar Law
It is against the law to put tomatoes in clam chowder.

Massachusetts is one of the smallest states, but there are more people living there than in any other New England state. Most of its inhabitants live in the greater Boston area.

The cranberry bogs (shallow marshes on Cape Cod) make Massachusetts the nation's largest cranberry producer. Farmers flood the bogs each winter to protect the crops from the cold.

Benjamin Franklin, John Adams, and Paul Revere were all born in Massachusetts.

The African Meeting House on Joy Street in Boston was the first church built by free blacks. It was built in 1806.

Literature

Boston Tea Party
by Pamela Duncan Edwards
(Putnam)

This book is written in the pattern of *This is the House that Jack Built*. Set in Massachusetts, it offers a perfect understanding of what the Boston Tea Party was and why it happened. The book contains a time line (displayed on a stars and stripes ribbon) that covers the period from 1763 to 1783. ◎≋ **Historical Fiction**

Comet's Nine Lives
by Jan Brett
(Puffin)

Comet lives on Nantucket Island and uses up eight of his nine lives finding the perfect place to settle. When he meets up with a beautiful green-eyed cat in the lighthouse, he knows he has found his home.
◎≋ **Current Events**

Letting Swift River Go
by Jane Yolen
(Econo-Clad Books)

Based on the author's past, this book tells the story of the drowning of the Swift River valley towns in western Massachusetts, during the period of 1927–1946. The demise of these towns was necessary in order to build the Quabbin Reservoir to provide water for the large cities that had grown up in the area. The text is nostalgic and lyrical, and the illustrations by Barbara Cooney are beautiful. ◎≋ **Historical Fiction**

Paul Revere's Ride
by Henry Wadsworth
Longfellow
(Puffin)

Ted Rand has put this famous poem, about Paul Revere's ride across the Massachusetts countryside, in book form with his unique illustrations. There's an additional information page about Paul Revere's ride at the back of the book. ◎≋ **Historical Fiction**

Shaker Hearts
by Ann Turner
(HarperCollins)

Hands to work, hearts to God is the Shaker motto, and it is repeated on each page of this book that depicts life in a Shaker village. The author starts the book with a two-page note about the Shaker faith and its beginnings in America. The book itself is based upon the research she did in Hancock Shaker Village in Massachusetts.
◎≋ **Cultural/Historical Fiction**

Three Young Pilgrims
by Cheryl Harness
(Simon & Schuster)

This story follows the life of a Pilgrim family from their voyage on the Mayflower through that first harsh winter at Plymouth Plantation. One of the little girls grows up to be the last surviving passenger from the Mayflower. At the end of the book, there is a passenger list from the Mayflower that designates the passengers as Pilgrims or Strangers.
◎≋ **Historical Fiction**

Michigan

State Flag

Wish You Were Here!

Capital
Lansing

Population
9,938,444

Statehood Date
January 26, 1837

State Number
26th

Motto
If You Seek a Pleasant Peninsula, Look About You

Song
"Michigan, My Michigan"

Bird
Robin

Flower
Apple Blossom

Tree
Western White Pine

Related State Facts & Trivia

Peculiar Law
It was illegal to hitch a crocodile to a fire hydrant.

Michigan leads the nation in the production of motor vehicles and motor vehicle parts.

Lake Michigan is the only one of the five Great Lakes to lie entirely within the boundaries of the United States. It is the third largest of the Great Lakes and the fifth largest freshwater lake in the world.

Michigan was a leader in the development of plank roads. Plank roads were made by laying down long boards called sleepers or stringers and then laying planks of wood across them. The planks would be 8 to 16 ft (2.5 to 5 m) long and 3 to 4 in (7.5 to 10 cm) thick. Ditches on either side of the road would provide drainage and keep the roads dry. To pay for building the plank roads, travelers paid a toll.

Literature

Betty Doll
by Patricia Polacco
(Penguin Putnam)

The author tells a heartrending tale from her past about a special doll that belonged to her mother. The doll and the accompanying note, both intended for Patricia, don't show up until years after her mother dies. ◎≈ **General Fiction**

The Legend of Mackinac Island
by Kathy-jo Wargin
(Sleeping Bear Press)

In addition to an absolutely beautiful legend about the origination of Mackinac Island in the Great Lakes region of Michigan, this book features paintings by Gijsbert van Frankenhuyzen. ◎≈ **Legend**

The Legend of Sleeping Bear
by Kathy-jo Wargin
(Sleeping Bear Press)

This book presents the legend about the origination of the Manitou Islands, near Sleeping Bear Bay, in Lake Michigan. The story begins in the woods of Wisconsin, where a mother bear and her two cubs are living, happily, until they are frightened away by a forest fire. They attempt to escape by swimming across Lake Michigan. It is a sad but touching tale. ◎≈ **Legend**

The Log Cabin Quilt
by Ellen Howard
(Holiday House)

When Elvirey and her family leave the Carolinas for the Michigan woods, she has no idea what hardships they will face. She only knows that her heart is heavy at the thought of leaving her mother's grave and her mother's belongings behind. Her granny insists on bringing her bag of quilting scraps with them, and something special happens that makes their new home really seem like home. ◎≈ **Historical Fiction**

Mr. Lincoln's Way
by Patricia Polacco
(Philomel)

Mr. Lincoln is a very special principal, indeed. His way is a way that can reach a little boy who seems destined for a life of unhappiness. This delightful and uplifting tale comes from the author's memories of her elementary school days in Michigan. ◎≈ **General Fiction**

My Rotten Redheaded Older Brother
by Patricia Polacco
(Simon & Schuster)

The author's account of her childhood on her grandparents' farm in Union City, Michigan, results in a funny, touching story of sibling rivalry. It seems to little Patricia that her older brother can outdo her at everything. She learns at the end of the story just how special older brothers can be. ◎≈ **General Fiction**

Thundercake
by Patricia Polacco
(Philomel)

Ever heard of Thundercake? This book comes complete with a recipe for the best Thundercake you will ever eat. Besides being delicious, this special cake can help you pass the time during a thunderstorm. As the author discovered with her grandma in Michigan, a person won't even have time to be afraid. ◎≈ **General Fiction**

Minnesota

State Flag

Capital
St. Paul

Population
4,919,479

Statehood Date
May 11, 1858

State Number
32nd

Motto
The Star of the North

Song
"Hail! Minnesota"

Bird
Common Loon

Flower
Pink and White Lady's Slipper

Tree
Norway Pine

USA

Related State Facts & Trivia

Rochester, Minnesota, is the home of the internationally famous Mayo Clinic, known for its achievements in the field of medicine.

Peculiar Law
It was illegal for a woman to appear on the street dressed as Santa Claus.

Minnesota is a leading state in the computer industry, and some of the world's foremost manufacturers have high-tech plants in the Twin Cities.

Austin, Minnesota, is home to Hormel Foods, which makes Spam. Every summer they sponsor Spam Days to celebrate the canned meat.

Paul Bunyan and his blue ox Babe are larger-than-life legends from the logging period of Minnesota's history. Paul Bunyan was a giant woodsman who was capable of many feats. His footprints became the 10,000 lakes, and one swing of his ax could cut down a whole forest.

Literature

Copy Me, Copycub
by Richard Edwards
(HarperCollins)

Set in the northwoods, this is a sweet story of a mother bear who teaches her cub how to live and survive in the woods. ◎≈ **Science**

**John Blair and
the Great Hinckley Fire**
by Josephine Nobisso
(Houghton Mifflin)

This book tells how a brave African American porter helped save many lives when the train on which he was working was caught up in the terrible firestorm near Hinkley, Minnesota, in 1894. ◎≈ **Historical Fiction**

Mississippi Going North
by Sanna Anderson Baker
(Albert Whitman)

The author describes the sights during a canoe trip north from the headwaters of the Mississippi River through remote natural settings. ◎≈ **Geography**

Up North at the Cabin
by Marsha Wilson Chall
(HarperCollins)

A narrative, prose poem combined with beautiful watercolor illustrations makes this a beautiful collection of summer memories from the northwoods. ◎≈ **General Fiction**

**Washing the
Willow Tree Loon**
by Jacqueline Briggs Martin
(Simon & Schuster)

This is a touching, informative book about cleaning and rehabilitating oiled birds. The loon is Minnesota's state bird. ◎≈ **Science**

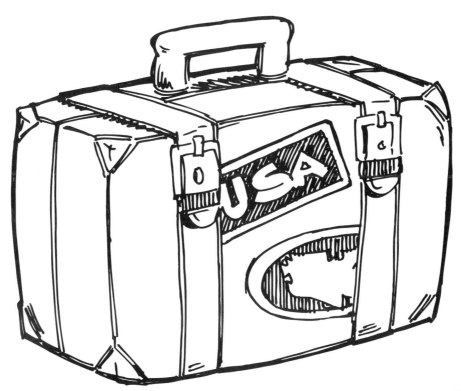

Mississippi

State Flag

Wish You Were Here!

Capital
Jackson

Population
2,844,658

Statehood Date
December 10, 1817

State Number
20th

Motto
By Valor and Arms

USA

Song
"Go, Mississippi!"

Bird
Mockingbird

Flower
Magnolia

Tree
Magnolia

Related State Facts & Trivia

Peculiar Law
It was illegal to soap railroad tracks.

Fishing is an important industry in Mississippi. Catches include, catfish, shrimp, menhaden, red snappers, oysters, and carp.

The delta is the fertile flood plain between the Mississippi and Yazoo Rivers. Paddle steamers took passengers and goods along the Mississippi River. Today, similar boats carry mostly tourists.

The name Mississippi comes from an Indian word meaning "Father of Waters."

Literature

Bristle Face
by Zachary Ball
(Holiday House)

After running away from his brutal uncle's Mississippi home, Jase meets a stray dog who is as funny-looking as he is loving. When the two enter Lute Swank's general store, they know they've found another friend—and maybe even a home. ◎≋ **General Fiction**

Everywhere in Mississippi
by Laurie Parker
(Quail Ridge Press)

This is the story of a man in search of his lost dog, Skippy. His journey across the state takes him through over 300 Mississippi cities, towns, and communities, all ingeniously integrated into this twisting, turning tale. ◎≋ **Geography/General Fiction**

Flood: Wrestling With the Mississippi
by Patricia Lauber
(Publishers Group West)

This is a stunning photo essay about the flooding of the Mississippi River in 1993. It includes a discussion of the river's need to expand and humanity's need to control the river. ◎≋ **Science/Historical Fiction**

Freedom School, Yes!
by Amy Littlesugar
(Philomel)

When their house is attacked because her mother volunteered to take in the young white woman who has come to teach black students at the Freedom School, Jolie is afraid, but she overcomes her fear after learning the value of education. ◎≋ **Historical Fiction**

Freedom Summer
by Deborah Wiles
(Atheneum Books)

In the summer of 1964, civil rights workers in Mississippi organized something they called "Freedom Summer." This book is a fictionalized account, based on real events in the author's life, of some of the things that happened that summer. Two best friends, one white and one black, find they can do almost everything together. ◎≋ **Historical Fiction**

Granddaddy's Gift
by Margaree King Mitchell
(BridgeWater Books)

When her grandfather registers to vote while living in segregated Mississippi, a girl begins to understand why he insists that she attend school. ◎≋ **Historical Fiction**

Love, Ruby Lavender
by Deborah Wiles
(Harcourt)

This is a humorous chapter book about a spunky nine-year-old during a summer of growing up. The story is set in Halleluia, Mississippi, "Population: 400 Good Friendly Folks And A Few Old Soreheads," and has a young hero readers can root for. ◎≋ **General Fiction (Humor)**

Missouri

State Flag

Wish You Were Here!

Capital
Jefferson City

Population
5,595,211

Statehood Date
August 10, 1821

State Number
24th

Motto
The Welfare of the People Shall Be the Supreme Law

Song
"Missouri Waltz"

Bird
Bluebird

Flower
Hawthorn

Tree
Flowering Dogwood

USA

Related State Facts & Trivia

Peculiar Law

A man must have a permit to shave.

Missouri played a leading role as the gateway to the west. St. Joseph, Missouri, was the eastern starting point for the Pony Express, and both the Santa Fe and Oregon Trails began in Independence, Missouri.

David Rice Atchison, a Missouri native, held the office of president of the United States for one day in 1849. The terms of President James K. Polk and Vice President George Dallas officially expired at noon on Sunday, March 4. President-elect Zachary Taylor, a very religious man, refused to take the presidential oath on a Sunday. Senator Atchison, then president pro tem of the Senate, thus served as president of the United States from noon on March 4 until 11:30 a.m on March 5, 1849.

Mark Twain was born Samuel Clemens in a two-room cabin in 1835. He grew up in the town of Hannibal, which he made famous in his book *The Adventures of Tom Sawyer*.

Literature

A Family Apart (The Orphan Train Adventures #1)
by Joan Lowery Nixon
(Bantam Books)

When their mother can no longer support them, six siblings are sent by the Students' Aid Society of New York City to live with farm families in Missouri in 1860. This is the first book in a series. (A more detailed but adult-oriented nonfiction book is *Orphan Trains to Missouri* by Michael D. Patrick from the University of Missouri Press.) ◎≋ **Historical Fiction**

Front Porch Stories: At the One-Room School
by Eleanor E. Tate
(Bantam Books)

Twelve-year-old Margie and her younger cousin forget their boredom when Margie's father entertains them with stories about people and events in their small Missouri town's past. ◎≋ **General Fiction**

Jesse James: Legendary Outlaw
by Roger A. Bruns
(Enslow Publishers)

This book traces the life of the renowned bandit from his childhood in Missouri through his years as a guerilla fighter and an outlaw. It explores the development of his legend and the romanticizing of his illegal deeds. ◎≋ **Biography**

New Dawn on Rocky Ridge (Little House Series: The Rocky Ridge Years)
by Roger Lea MacBride
(HarperCollins)

While living on the Rocky Ridge Farm in Missouri, 13-year-old Rose Wilder celebrates the turn of the twentieth century and begins to wonder about her future. ◎≋ **Historical Fiction**

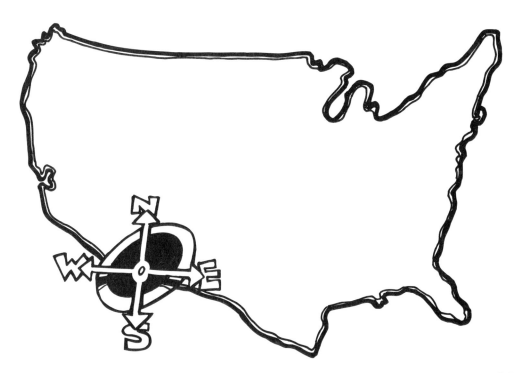

Montana

State Flag

Capital
Helena

Population
902,195

Statehood Date
November 8, 1889

State Number
41st

Motto
Gold and Silver

Song
"Montana"

Bird
Western Meadowlark

Flower
Bitterroot

Tree
Ponderosa Pine

Related State Facts & Trivia

Peculiar Law
It is illegal for a wife to open her husband's mail.

Montana is the fourth largest state with the forty-fourth largest population.

The major Indian Wars (1867–1877) included the famous 1876 Battle of the Little Big Horn, better known as Custer's Last Stand, in which Cheyenne and Sioux war parties killed George A. Custer and more than 200 of his men in southeastern Montana.

Jeannette Rankin, a Montana Republican, became the first woman to serve in Congress in 1917. The social worker was born near Missoula in 1880. She opposed the U.S. entry into World War I, cast the only vote against entering World War II, and later spoke out against participating in the Korean War. She died in 1973.

Literature

Brave Wolf and the Thunderbird: Tales of the People
by Medicine Crow
(Abbeville Press)

While hunting, Brave Wolf is snatched by a huge Thunderbird and taken to her nest on a high cliff so he can protect her chicks from a monster. ◎≋ **Legend**

Buffalo Days
by Diane Hoyt-Goldsmith
(Holiday House)

This book describes life on a Crow Indian reservation in Montana and the importance these tribes place on buffalo, which are once again thriving in areas where the Crow live. ◎≋ **Cultural**

Cowboy Charlie
by Jeanette Winter
(Harcourt Brace)

The author presents a biography of Charles Marion Russell in story form in this delightful book. When he was a little boy, he dreamed of being a cowboy and sleeping under the stars. At 15 years of age, he moved to Montana with a family friend, and his dreams came true. As a young adult, he started sketching and painting everything he saw and became a famous painter. ◎≋ **Biography**

Crow Students and Elders Talk Together
by E. Barrie Kavasch
(Powerkids Press)

This book explores the culture and traditions of the Crow Indians through the voices of a young girl, her father, and several other older people. ◎≋ **Cultural**

Where the Bald Eagles Gather
by Dorothy Hinshaw Patent
(Clarion Books)

Students will enjoy the vivid description—in text and photographs—of the annual gathering of bald eagles in Glacier National Park and of a wildlife research project to study the life cycle of our national bird. ◎≋ **Science**

Whitefish Will Rides Again
by Arthur Yorinks
(HarperCollins)

This is a Wild West tale from Whitefish, Montana. This fun and far-fetched story conjures up the kind of excitement that only a true cowboy story can. There's a good guy, Whitefish Will, and a bad guy, Bart. Guess who wears the white hat and who wears the black hat? ◎≋ **General Fiction**

Wolf at the Door
by Barbara Corcoran
(Maxwell Macmillan International)

Living in the shadow of her beautiful and talented younger sister, Lee cares for a wolf pack that needs protection from cattle ranchers. ◎≋ **General Fiction**

Nebraska

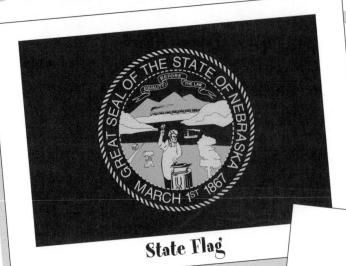

State Flag

ish You
Were Here!

Capital
Lincoln

Population
1,711,263

Statehood Date
March 1, 1867

State Number
37th

Motto
Equality Before the Law

USA

Song
"Beautiful Nebraska"

Bird
Western Meadowlark

Flower
Goldenrod

Tree
Cottonwood

Related State Facts & Trivia

Peculiar Law
It is illegal to picnic in the same place twice within a 30-day period.

The Frisbee® was invented in Lincoln, Nebraska.

KOOL-AID® originated in Hastings, Nebraska. The seven original KOOL-AID flavors were cherry, lemon-lime, grape, orange, root beer, strawberry, and raspberry.

In 1937, Nebraska became the only state in the Union to have a unicameral (one-house) legislature. Members are elected to it without party designation.

Gerald R. Ford was born in Omaha on July 14th, 1913. He was the only president who was not elected to office. Ford was vice president to President Richard Nixon and was appointed to his office when President Nixon resigned.

Literature

Dandelions
by Eve Bunting
(Harcourt)

This sweet story is about a family moving west to the Nebraska Territory and the mixed feelings they share within their family. Zoe, the little girl, says that she has never seen her father so happy or her mother so sad. Leaving Illinois and her grandparents' farm was hard, but, in time, Nebraska becomes home. ◎≈ **Historical Fiction**

The Huckabuck Family and How They Raised Popcorn in Nebraska and Quit and Came Back
by Carl Sandburg
(Farrar, Strauss & Giroux)

This zany and silly book is about a family that takes off for Nebraska to grow corn and decides to come home. It's not too silly to seem funny, especially to young students. ◎≈ **General Fiction**

The Mud Pony
retold by Caron Lee Cohen
(Scholastic)

A young Indian boy wishes for his own pony. Finally, he makes one out of mud during a dream. When he awakens, he finds the mud pony has come to life. He grows up to be the chief of his tribe. This legend could apply to many states, but the author mentions Nebraska in her acknowledgements. ◎≈ **Legend**

Prairie Songs
by Pam Conrad
(Harper & Row)

Louisa's life in a loving pioneer family on the Nebraska prairie is altered by the arrival of a new doctor and his wife. ◎≈ **Historical Fiction**

Nevada

State Flag

Capital
Carson City

Population
1,998,257

Statehood Date
October 31, 1864

State Number
36th

Motto
All for Our Country

Song
"Home Means Nevada"

Bird
Mountain Bluebird

Flower
Sagebrush

Tree
Single-leaf Pinon

Related State Facts & Trivia

Peculiar Law
It was illegal to drive camels on to main highways.

Nevada was made famous by the discovery of the fabulous Comstock Lode in 1859. Its mines have produced large quantities of gold, silver, copper, lead, zinc, mercury, barite, and tungsten.

Hoover Dam, near Las Vegas, stands at the head of the artificial lake it created, Lake Mead. The lake provides water and power for Las Vegas. It is a popular lake with both fishermen and tourists.

Nevada is the driest state in the nation with an average annual rainfall of only about 7 in (18 cm). The wettest part of the state receives about 40 in (1 m) of precipitation per year, while the driest spot has less than 4 in (10 cm) per year.

Literature

Alice Rose and Sam
by Kathryn Lasky
(Hyperion Press)

This chapter book is set in Nevada and is loosely based on the life of Samuel Clemens. ◎≈ **Historical Fiction**

The Runaways
by Zilpha Keatley Snyder
(Delacorte Press Books)

Twelve-year-old Dani hates living in the small desert town of Rattler Springs, Nevada, but her plans to run away get complicated when a pesky young boy and an imaginative new girl decide they want to go along. An exciting desert drama results when the three attempt to put the plan into action. The book is set in the 1950s, and the dying town and desperate people are very real. ◎≈ **General Fiction**

**Sarah Winnemucca:
Paiute Native American
Indian Stories**
by Mary F. Morrow
(Raintree Publishers)

The author recounts the life story of the influential Paiute woman who fought for justice and a better life for her people. ◎≈ **Biography**

Sierra
by Diane Siebert
(HarperCollins)

A lyrical text and gorgeous paintings by Wendell Minor accompany the reader on a trip through the Sierra Nevada Mountains. ◎≈ **Geography**

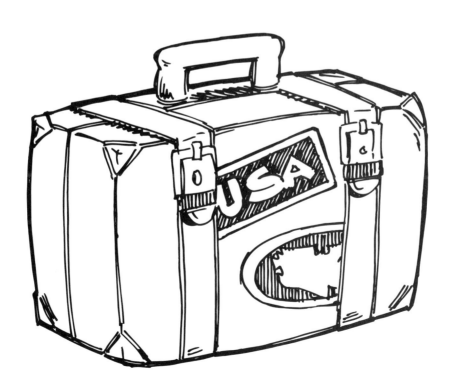

New Hampshire

State Flag

Wish You Were Here!

Capital
Concord

Population
1,235,786

Statehood Date
June 21, 1788

State Number
9th

Motto
Live Free or Die

Song
"Old New Hampshire"

Bird
Purple Finch

Flower
Purple Lilac

Tree
White Birch

Related State Facts & Trivia

Peculiar Law
You cannot sell the clothes you are wearing to pay off a gambling debt.

As leaders in the revolutionary cause, New Hampshire delegates received the honor of being the first to vote for the Declaration of Independence on July 4, 1776.

New Hampshire is the only state that ever played host at the formal conclusion of a foreign war. In 1905, Portsmouth was the scene of the treaty ending the Russo-Japanese War.

Franklin Pierce was the 14th president of the United States. He was born in New Hampshire and served in the state legislature from 1829 to 1833. He was known for his ability to compromise and was trusted by the South during the period leading up to the Civil War.

Literature

The Bear That Heard Crying
by Natalie Kinsey-Warnock
(Dutton)

This book is based on the true story of a little girl who is lost in the New Hampshire woods in 1783. It seems hopeless that anyone will be able to fine her, but a stranger passing through does just that. Once she is home safe and sound, she tells an amazing story. ◎≋ **Historical Fiction**

Christa McAuliffe:
Teacher in Space
by Corinne J. Naden
(The Millbrook Press)

The first private American citizen chosen to go on a space flight, Christa McAuliffe, lost her life when the Challenger exploded just after liftoff. This book describes her special interest in the space program. ◎≋ **Biography**

A Gathering of Days
by Joan W. Blos
(Scribner)

The journal of a 14-year-old girl, set in the 1830s and kept the last year she lived on the family farm, records daily events in her small New Hampshire town, her father's remarriage, and the death of her best friend. ◎≋ **Historical Fiction**

I Live in a Town
by Stasia Ward Kehoe
(Rosen Publishing Group)

An eight-year-old boy who lives in a small town in New Hampshire describes life in his rural community, including its homes, schools, town meetings, orchards, and special days. ◎≋ **Current Events**

Lucy's Summer
by Donald Hall
(Harcourt Brace)

For Lucy Wells, who lives on a farm in New Hampshire, the summer of 1910 is filled with helping her mother can fruits and vegetables, enjoying the Fourth of July celebration, and participating in many other activities. ◎≋ **Historical Fiction**

Pinkham's Notch
by Carol Hayes
(Peter Randall Publisher)

This is the story of Daniel Pinkham, a young farmer in the town of Adams (now Jackson), New Hampshire, who attempted to build the first road there. Woven through the text is the story of how the Border Wars between southern Canada and our northeastern states affected the area's residents. ◎≋ **Historical Fiction**

A River Ran Wild
by Lynn Cherry
(Harcourt)

This is a true story about the discovery, by the Indians, of the Nashua River Valley in Nashua, New Hampshire. The river was beautiful until it was polluted during the Industrial Revolution. Eventually, the river was saved by a group of hardworking people. This book is an environmental history of how those people, working toward the same purpose, were successful in their efforts to save the river. ◎≋ **Geography**

New Jersey

State Flag

Wish You Were Here!

Capital
Trenton

Population
8,414,350

Statehood Date
December 18, 1787

State Number
3rd

Motto
Liberty and Prosperity

Song
None

Bird
American Goldfinch

Flower
Purple Violet

Tree
Red Oak

Related State Facts & Trivia

Peculiar Law
It was illegal to delay or detain a homing pigeon.

The state seashell is the knobbed whelk because it is found on all the state's beaches and bays.

Modern paleontology, the science of studying dinosaur fossils, began in 1858 with the discovery of the first nearly complete skeleton of a dinosaur in Haddonfield, New Jersey. The Hadrosaurus is the official New Jersey state dinosaur.

Tomatoes used to be considered poisonous. (They belong to the nightshade family.) On September 26, 1820, Robert Gibbon Johnson of Salem, New Jersey, once and for all proved that tomatoes were nonpoisonous and safe for consumption when he stood on the steps of the Salem courthouse and bravely consumed an entire basket of tomatoes without keeling over or suffering any ill effects whatsoever. His grandstanding attracted a crowd of people who were certain he was committing public suicide. Johnson's actions that day got him a lot of attention and gave New Jersey its most popular vegetable. This display of courage is reenacted every year during Market Street Days in Salem on the third Saturday in August.

Literature

The 18 Penny Goose
by Sally M. Walker
(HarperCollins)

Eight-year-old Letty attempts to save her pet goose from marauding British soldiers in New Jersey during the Revolutionary War. ◎≈ **Historical Fiction**

The Battlefield Ghost
by Margery Cuyler
(Scholastic)

When fourth grader John and his sister Lisa move into an old house in Princeton, New Jersey, they find it haunted by the ghost of a Hessian soldier from the Revolutionary War and try to reunite him with the ghost of his beloved horse. ◎≈ **General Fiction**

Boss of the Plains
by Laurie Carlson
(DK Publishing)

Until 1860, there was no such thing as a cowboy hat. It was then that John Batterson Stetson invented the cowboy hat in his family's hat maker's shop in Orange, New Jersey. This book tells the story of John Stetson and his hat. ◎≈ **Historical Fiction**

Crossing the Delaware
by Louise Peacock
(Atheneum Books)

The harsh winter of 1776 found the American soldiers cold, tired, and hungry. The British troops were well fed and rested. What could George Washington do? He made a tough decision: attack. That meant crossing the Delaware River into Trenton, New Jersey. This book brings that night vividly to life. ≈ **Historical Fiction**

The Hindenburg
by Patrick O'Brien
(Henry Holt and Company)

This book describes the development and early flights of airships and the disastrous crash of the Hindenburg at an airfield in New Jersey in 1937. ◎≈ **Historical Nonfiction**

The Seventeenth Student
by Dorothy Marie Rice
(Linnet Books)

This is an oral history of the seventeenth student of black sharecroppers who describes her life in Virginia and New Jersey during the Depression. ◎≈ **Biography**

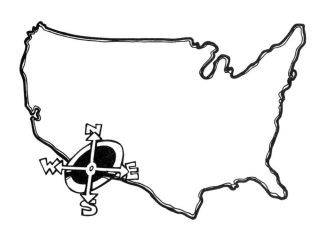

New Mexico

State Flag

Wish You Were Here!

Capital
Santa Fe

Population
1,819,046

Statehood Date
January 6, 1912

State Number
47th

Motto
It Grows As It Goes

USA

Song
"O, Fair New Mexico"

Bird
Roadrunner

Flower
Yucca Flower

Tree
Piñon Pine

Related State Facts & Trivia

Peculiar Law
It was illegal to climb a building to get a free view of a ball game.

New Mexico has two state vegetables: the chili and the pinto bean (made into frijole). In 1965, the legislative debate ended when it was decided that the chile and frijole were inseparable and both should be the state vegetable. A combination of the vitamin-rich chile and the high-protein frijole will give a memorable dining experience.

New Mexico is one of the U.S. leaders in output of uranium and potassium salts. Copper, silver, iron, and lead are also mined in New Mexico. Much of the state's wealth comes from oil and natural gas.

New Mexico's distinctive insignia (found on the state flag) is the Zia Sun symbol, which originated with the Indians of the Zia Pueblo in ancient times. Its design reflects their tribal philosophy, with its wealth of pantheistic spiritualism that teaches the basic harmony of all things in the universe.

Literature

Alejandro's Gift
by Richard E. Albert
(Chronicle Books)

A lonely man, living in his small house in the desert, works hard to provide an inviting oasis for the desert animals. He thinks he is giving them a gift, but realizes that he is the one who is receiving a gift: their company. There is a glossary of desert plants and animals, complete with illustrations, at the back of the book.
◎≈ **General Fiction/Information**

The Boy Who Made Dragonfly: A Zuñi Myth
by Tony Hillerman
(Harper & Row)

This book retells a Zuñi myth in which a young boy and his sister gain the wisdom that makes them leaders of their people through the intercession of a dragonfly. ◎≈ **Legend**

Carlos and the Cornfield/ Carlos Y La Milpa De Maiz
by Jan Romero Stevens
(Northland Publishing)

When he sees the results of not following his father's instructions on the proper way to plant corn, a young boy tries to make things right. ◎≈ **General Fiction**

The Girl Who Chased Away Sorrow: The Diary of Sarah Nita, a Navajo Girl, New Mexico, 1864
(Dear America series)
by Ann Warren Turner
(Scholastic)

This story details the journey of Sarah Nita who is forced by American soldiers on the Long Walk. Sarah tells fables to pass the time and keep her spirits up. ◎≈ **Historical Fiction/Cultural**

Lewis and Papa
by Barbara Joosse
(Chronicle Books)

After hearing stories about the adventures on the Santa Fe Trail, Lewis and his father leave their home on the Wisconsin River and join a wagon train traveling to Santa Fe, New Mexico. They find more than excitement on the trip … they find a new element to their relationship, as Lewis changes from a boy to a man. The illustrations are beautiful and creatively presented. ◎≈ **Historical Fiction/Cultural**

Memories of Cibola: Stories from New Mexico Villages
by Abe M. Pena
(University of New Mexico Press)

These stories of Hispanic lives and experiences between the 1920s and the 1950s speak to such universal themes as coming of age, striking out on one's own, and joining family and neighbors to celebrate good times and to aid them in overcoming hardships.
◎≈ **Historical Fiction/Cultural**

Old Father Story Teller
by Pablita Velarde
(Clear Light Publishers)

There are six stories in the book, each with several of Velarde's fabulous paintings. ◎≈ **Cultural**

New York

State Flag

Capital
Albany

Population
18,976,457

Statehood Date
July 26, 1788

State Number
11th

Motto
Ever Upward

Song
"I Love New York"

Bird
Bluebird

Flower
Rose

Tree
Sugar Maple

USA

ish You
re Here!

Related State Facts & Trivia

Peculiar Law
It used to be illegal to ring the doorbell and disturb the occupant of a house.

New York was the first state to preserve a historic site (Washington's Headquarters at Newburgh), establish a state park (Niagara Reservation), and declare land "forever wild" (the Adirondack and Catskill forest preserves) in a state constitution.

The term "The Big Apple" was coined by touring jazz musicians of the 1930s who used the slang expression "apple" for any town or city. Therefore, to play New York City is to play the big time.

New York was the birthplace of Franklin Delano Roosevelt. He was born January 30, 1882, and became the 32nd president in 1933. He reformed the banking system, helped farmers, and created jobs through large public projects. He was greatly assisted by his wife, Eleanor.

Literature

The Arrow over the Door
by Joseph Bruchac
(Dial Books)

Fourteen-year-old Samuel Russell is a Quaker who vows to defend his family. Stands Straight is an Abenaki boy whose mother and brother were murdered by white men. The boys' voices alternate to tell their story, which is based on an actual incident that took place in 1777. This book makes an excellent read-aloud or chapter book for advanced readers. The author provides background about the meeting of these two cultures. ◎≈ **Historical Fiction/Cultural**

Brooklyn Dodger Days
by Richard Rosenblum
(Maxwell Macmillan)

This book is pure New York, circa 1946, as it recreates a baseball game between the Brooklyn Dodgers and their rivals, the New York Giants. It comes complete with descriptions of Ebbetts Field, subways, street vendors, and the hustle and bustle that place the reader right on the streets of New York City. ◎≈ **Historical Fiction**

Casey Over There
by Staton Rabin
(Harcourt)

World War I is underway, and Aubrey's older brother, Casey, joins up. Aubrey sits atop the Ferris wheel at Coney Island and misses his brother. Finally, Aubrey writes a letter to Uncle Sam, asking him to send his brother home. The muted, sepia-tone illustrations really give this book an authentic feeling. ◎≈ **Historical Fiction**

The Gardener
by Sarah Stewart
(Farrar, Straus & Giroux)

This Depression-era book tells the story of a little girl who is sent from out west to live in New York City with her uncle who owns a bakery. The book is a series of letters she sends home, shedding light on life in the city without ground to plant flowers and with an uncle who doesn't smile. ◎≈ **Historical Fiction**

Jamaica Louise James
by Amy Hest
(Candlewick Press)

Jamaica is eight years old and lives in New York City with her mother and grandmother. Her "grammy" works at the 86th Street subway station. Jamaica decides to decorate the walls of the station with her paintings as a surprise for her grammy's birthday, and she ends up having a brass plaque with her name on it permanently mounted on the wall. ◎≈ **General Fiction**

The Pushcart War
by Jean Merrill
(Yearling Books)

This fictional tale about a war between pushcarts and the trucks who vie for space on the New York City streets contains little historical information about New York, but it retains all the flavor of the city and characters who live there. A humorous chapter book for the more fluent reader or read-aloud, this book provides fodder for discussions about justice, nonviolent methods of rebellion, and the problems of city traffic. ◎≈ **General Fiction**

North Carolina

State Flag

Wish You Were Here!

Capital
Raleigh

Population
8,049,313

Statehood Date
November 21, 1789

State Number
12th

Motto
To Be Rather
Than to Seem

Song
"The Old North State"

Bird
Cardinal

Flower
Flowering Dogwood

Tree
Pine

USA

Related State Facts & Trivia

Peculiar Law

It is against the law for cats and dogs to fight.

Students at a Wilson County school petitioned the North Carolina General Assembly for the establishment of the sweet potato as the Official State Vegetable. Their assignment led to the creation of the newest state symbol. North Carolina is the largest producer of sweet potatoes in the nation, harvesting over 4 billion lbs (1.8 billion kg) of the vegetable in 1989. The sweet potato is high in vitamins A and C and low in fat and was grown in North Carolina before the European colonization of North America.

North Carolina is one of the homes to the black bear. The state's large areas of forest are an ideal environment for the bear. The black bear is the smallest and most common type of bear in the U.S.

In 1903, the Wright Brothers made the first successful powered flight by man at Kill Devil Hill near Kitty Hawk. The Wright Memorial at Kitty Hawk now commemorates their achievement.

Literature

Appalachia
by Cynthia Rylant
(Harcourt)

This book describes the quiet life in the mountains. ◎≈ **Cultural**

Red Wolf Country
by Jonathan London
(Dutton)

Beautifully illustrated by Daniel San Souci, this is a story about two red wolves. They hunt together and travel together, looking for the perfect den that will offer the protection they will need when spring arrives and their pups are born. The author includes an afterword that gives information about the declining red wolf population in this country. ◎≈ **General Fiction/Information**

Sody Sallyratus
retold by Teri Sloat
(Dutton)

Set in the Appalachian Mountains, this folktale is about a family who goes, one at a time, into the village to get baking soda for some special biscuits and crosses paths with a big black bear. The repetition is typical of most folktales and makes for a great read-aloud. ◎≈ **Legend**

The Year of the Perfect Christmas Tree
by Gloria Houston
(Dial Books)

Set in the Appalachian Mountains this story describes how Ruthie's pa is called away to war, making things very tough for Ruthie and her ma. Still, it's their turn to provide the Christmas tree for the village church on Christmas Eve. This is where the tale of character, love, honor, and respect begins . . . and ends. ◎≈ **Historical Fiction**

North Dakota

State Flag

Wish You Were Here!

Capital
Bismarck

Population
642,200

Statehood Date
November 2, 1889

State Number
39th

Motto
Liberty and Union, Now and
Forever, One and Inseparable

Song
"North Dakota Hymn"

Bird
Western Meadowlark

Flower
Wild Rose

Tree
American Elm

Related State Facts & Trivia

Peculiar Law
It used to be illegal for railroad engineers to take their engines home with them unless they carried a full crew.

North Dakota is the most rural of all the states, with farms covering more than 90% of the land. Wheat is the chief crop. North Dakota is second only to Kansas in wheat production. Other crops grown in North Dakota include barley, rye, and oats. The state is also home to beef and dairy cattle.

Farther from a moderating body of water than any other state, North Dakota is an extreme example of "continental climate." The temperatures range from −60°F (−50°C) to 120°F (50°C).

The Badlands of North Dakota are strange rock formations that are the result of millions of years of erosion by wind and water. Pioneers found the land difficult to cross and gave it the dramatic nickname.

Literature

Adopted by the Eagles:
A Plains Indian Story of
Friendship and Treachery
by Paul Goble
(Simon & Schuster)

Two friends go out hunting for horses—but only one returns—in this story based in the Lakota Indian tradition. ◎≋ **Legend**

Dances With Wolves:
A Story for Students
by James Howe
(Newmarket Press)

After the Civil War, an army officer is sent west and becomes deeply involved in the affairs of a Sioux Indian tribe. ◎≋ **Historical Fiction**

The Great Race: Of
the Birds and Animals
by Paul Goble
(Bradbury Press)

This is a retelling of the Cheyenne and Sioux myth about the Great Race, a contest called by the Creator to settle the question whether man or buffalo should have supremacy and thus become the guardians of Creation. ◎≋ **Legend**

Moonstick: The Seasons
of the Sioux
by Eve Bunting
(HarperCollins)

A young Dakota Indian boy describes the changes that come both in nature and in the life of his people with each new moon of the Sioux year. ◎≋ **Cultural/Information**

There Still Are Buffalo
by Ann Nolan Clark
(Ancient City Press)

On the plains of North Dakota, a baby buffalo is born. This is his story, growing from a young bull and eventually challenging the leader of the herd. ◎≋ **Science**

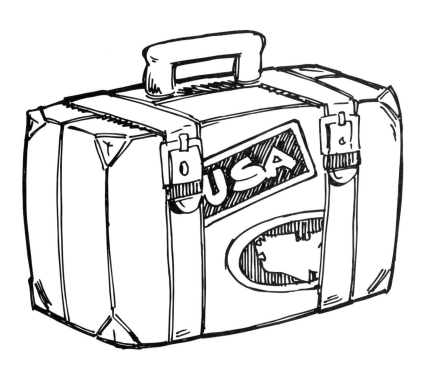

Ohio

State Flag

Capital
Columbus

Population
11,353,140

Statehood Date
March 1, 1803

State Number
17th

Motto
With God,
All Things are Possible

USA

Song
"Beautiful Ohio"

Bird
Cardinal

Flower
Scarlet Carnation

Tree
Buckeye

Related State Facts & Trivia

Peculiar Law
It is illegal to fish for whales on Sunday.

Ohio is home to artifacts of prehistoric Indian settlement. The Mound Builders created huge burial and effigy mounds and enclosures. They put well-crafted items such as copper breastplates, tools, shells, carved pipes, and ornaments made of grizzly bear teeth in the mounds. One example, Serpent Mound, is near Hillsboro.

Rider's Inn in Painesville, which is still open to guests today, was a stagecoach stop that became a station on the Underground Railroad.

Ohio ranks third in the U.S. in manufacturing. It is the largest producer of buses and trucks in the country and produces a high percentage of its automobiles, too.

Literature

The Bat Boy & His Violin
by Gavin Curtis
(Simon & Schuster)

Reginald loves to play the violin. His father is the manager of the Dukes, the worst team in the Negro National League. These two interests don't seem to be compatible, until something happens at a game in Cleveland, Ohio, that changes the way Reginald's pa will think about his fiddlin' forever. ◎≈ **General Fiction**

If I Were A Butterfly
by James Howe
(Harcourt)

Ever feel like an ugly cricket in the presence of a beautiful butterfly? This book, which got its beginnings in the Old Trail School in Bath, Ohio, tells the story of a sad cricket who gets advice from a wise spider. ◎≈ **Legend**

Shooting Star—Annie Oakley, the Legend
by Debbie Dadey
(Walker and Company)

A legend from the Wild West, Annie Oakley's story is a lot of fun. She traveled all over the country and the world, showing off her skill with a rifle; but she got her start in Darke County, Ohio, in 1860. ◎≈ **Biography**

Teammates
by Peter Golenbock
(Harcourt)

In 1947, the Brooklyn Dodgers traveled to Cincinnati, Ohio, to play a game against the Cincinnati Reds. Two members of that Dodger team were Jackie Robinson, the first black man to play major league baseball, and Pee Wee Reese, the Dodger shortstop most likely to lose his position to this new player. This book tells about an incident that happened that day that changed National League Baseball forever. ◎≈ **Biography**

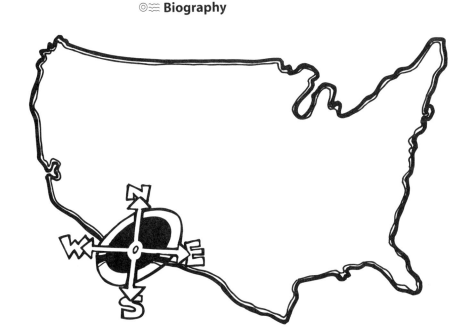

Oklahoma

State Flag

ish You
Were Here!

Capital
Oklahoma City

Population
3,450,654

Statehood Date
November 16, 1907

State Number
46th

Motto
Work Conquers All Things

Song
"Oklahoma"

Bird
Scissor-Tailed Flycatcher

Flower
Mistletoe

Tree
Redbud

Related State Facts & Trivia

Peculiar Law
It was illegal to catch whales in Oklahoma waters.

Oklahoma has the largest American Indian population of any state. Many of the 252,420 American Indians living in Oklahoma today are descendants from the original 67 tribes that inhabited Indian Territory.

On April 22, 1889, the first day homesteading was permitted, 50,000 people swarmed into the area. Those who tried to beat the noon starting gun were called Sooners, hence the state's nickname.

In the 1920s, Tulsa had more millionaires than any other city in the United States. Their wealth came from oil and other minerals mined around the city. To this day, Tulsa has excellent museums, performing arts centers, and medical facilities.

Literature

The Cowboy ABC
by Chris Demarest
(DK Publishing)

This ABC book of cowboy lingo, written in rhyme, leads students to predict the ending words. The illustrations are as fun as the text. The author hasn't given a specific setting, but it seems to fit nicely in Oklahoma where a lot of cowboys roamed the range. ◎≋ **Cultural**

The Flimflam Man
by Darleen Bailey Beard
(Farrar, Straus & Giroux)

In the summer of 1950, a con man comes to Wetumka, Oklahoma, to tell about his fabulous circus, and although he swindles the townspeople, two young girls grow from the experience. ◎≋ **General Fiction**

I Have Heard of a Land
by Joyce Carol Thomas
(HarperCollins)

This story describes the joys and hardships experienced by an African American pioneer woman who staked a claim for free land in the Oklahoma territory. ◎≋ **Historical Nonfiction**

Jingle Dancer
by Cynthia Leitich Smith
(Morrow Junior Books)

Jenna, a member of the Muscogee, or Creek, Nation, borrows jingles from the dresses of several friends and relatives so that she can perform the jingle dance at the powwow. This book includes a note about the jingle dance tradition and its regalia. ◎≋ **Historical Fiction**

One April Morning: Students Remember the Oklahoma City Bombing
by Nancy Lamb
(Lothrop, Lee & Shepard)

This book contains conversations with students from the Oklahoma City area about their feelings at the time of and following the bombing of the federal building. ◎≋ **Current Events**

Oregon

STATE OF OREGON

THE UNION

1859

State Flag

Wish You
Were Here!

Capital
Salem

Population
3,421,399

Statehood Date
February 14, 1859

State Number
33rd

Motto
She Flies with Her
Own Wings, The Union

Song
"Oregon, My Oregon"

Bird
Western Meadowlark

Flower
Oregon Grape

Tree
Douglas Fir

USA

Related State Facts & Trivia

Peculiar Law
It was illegal for a dead person to serve on a jury.

Pacific Ocean fishing is as important now to as it was to the Chinook tribe that first inhabited the region. Wild and farmed trout and salmon are sought by this industry.

The Oregon Trail stretches from Independence, Missouri, to The Dalles, on the northern Oregon border. It was an important route for settlers making their way west in the 1840s–1870s.

Oregon raises 99% of the country's hazelnuts.

Literature

Bess's Log Cabin Quilt
by D. Anne Love
(Holiday House)

With her father away and her mother ill with fever, ten-year-old Bess works hard on a log cabin quilt to save the family farm.
◎≋ **General Fiction**

I'm Sorry, Almira Ann
by Jane Kurtz
(Henry Holt and Company)

Eight-year-old Sarah's high spirits help make her family's long journey from Missouri to Oregon more bearable, though they do cause both her and her best friend, Almira Ann, some problems.
◎≋ **General Fiction**

Only Opal—The Diary of a Young Girl
by Barbara Cooney
(Philomel)

This is a true story about a little girl, Opal, who goes to live with a family in Oregon, upon the death of her parents. She has a hard life with her foster parents. Even though she faces a lot of sadness, she finds beauty and happiness in simple things. ◎≋ **Historical Nonfiction**

Pioneer Cat
by William H. Hooks
(Random House)

When a young pioneer girl smuggles a cat aboard the wagon train taking her family from Missouri to Oregon, it turns out to be the best thing she could have done. ◎≋ **Historical Fiction**

Roughing It on the Oregon Trail
by Diane Stanley
(HarperCollins)

Twins Liz and Lenny, along with their time-traveling grandmother, join a group of pioneers journeying west on the Oregon Trail in 1843.
◎≋ **Historical Fiction**

Westward Ho with Ollie Ox
by Melanie Richardson Dundy
(MDCT Publishing)

Invite students to come travel the Oregon Trail with Ollie Ox as their guide. Ollie, an ox who is pulling the covered wagon from Independence, Missouri, to Oregon, narrates the story.
◎≋ **Historical Fiction**

Pennsylvania

State Flag

Wish You Were Here!

Capital
Harrisburg

Population
12,281,054

Statehood Date
December 12, 1787

State Number
2nd

Motto
Virtue, Liberty, and Independence

Song
None

Bird
Ruffed Grouse

Flower
Mountain Laurel

Tree
Western Hemlock

Related State Facts & Trivia

Peculiar Law
In Philadelphia, you can't put pretzels in bags based on an Act of 1760.

Hershey, Pennsylvania is the home of the Hershey® Bar.

Philadelphia was the seat of the federal government almost continuously from 1776 to 1800. From 1790 to 1800, the city served as the nation's first capital.

The first settlers in the area were Dutch and Swedish, but in 1682 an English colony was founded by William Penn for an offshoot of Protestants known as the Quakers, who were seeking religious freedom. He founded Pennsylvania, which means "city of brotherly love" in Greek.

Pennsylvania dairy cows produce more than 10 billion lbs (4,536,000,000 kg) of milk every year.

Literature

Bewildered for Three Days
by Andrew Glass
(Holiday House)

This is an original tall tale about Daniel Boone's adventurous life growing up in Pennsylvania. It's also about bears and Indian pals, and it answers the question about why he never wore his coonskin cap. ◎≈ **Biography**

The Hatmaker's Sign
retold by Candace Fleming
(Orchard Books)

To help Thomas Jefferson accept the response of the Continental Congress to his draft of the Declaration of Independence, Benjamin Franklin tells the story of a hat maker and his sign. This is based on an actual conversation between these two great American statesmen. ◎≈ **Historical Fiction**

Just Plain Fancy
by Patricia Polacco
(Bantam Books)

Life in an Amish community in Pennsylvania is examined in this delightful story about a young girl, Naomi, who quite accidentally helps a peacock egg to hatch. Naomi and her little sister, Ruth, are afraid what might happen when the elders discover this fancy creature they have hidden away. ◎≈ **General Fiction**

Pioneer Church
by Carolyn Otto
(Henry Holt and Company)

This beautifully written and illustrated book focuses on the role churches have played in the history of our country. Early pioneer churches served as meeting halls, schools, hospitals, and places of worship. The story is based on an actual church that is located in Brickerville, Pennsylvania. ◎≈ **Historical Fiction**

Selina and the Bear Paw Quilt
by Barbara Smucker
(Crown Books)

A Mennonite family living in Pennsylvania is faced with a tough decision when the Civil War breaks out. Their religious beliefs forbid them from bearing arms or taking sides. They decide to go to Canada to avoid the religious persecution they would suffer. Selina can't bear to leave her home in Pennsylvania and, especially, her grandmother. A special quilt helps to ease the loneliness. ◎≈ **Historical Fiction**

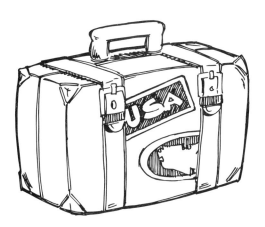

Rhode Island

State Flag

Wish You Were Here!

Capital
Providence

Population
1,048,319

Statehood Date
May 29, 1790

State Number
13th

Motto
Hope

Song
"Rhode Island, It's for Me"

Bird
Rhode Island Red

Flower
Purple Violet

Tree
Red Maple

Related State Facts & Trivia

Peculiar Law
It is considered an offense to throw pickle juice on a trolley.

The largest manufacturer of silverware in the world is in Providence.

French- and Italian-style mansions line a 3-mi (5-km) stretch of coastal Newport, Rhode Island. The owners (the Astors, Vanderbilts, and Belmonts) made their wealth from the industrialization of the 1800s.

Samuel Slater, the father of the American Industrial Revolution, built the first successful water-powered textile mill in Pawtucket in 1793.

Literature

Finding Providence—
The Story of Roger Williams
by Avi
(HarperCollins)

This is a beginning chapter book that can be easily read aloud at one sitting. It is the true story of the founding of Providence, Rhode Island. ◎≈ **Historical Nonfiction**

Mill
by David MacAulay
(Houghton Mifflin)

The mills described in this book are imaginary, but their planning, construction, and operation are quite typical of mills developed in New England throughout the nineteenth century. ◎≈ **Historical Fiction**

Sophie's Masterpiece
by Eileen Spinelli
(Simon & Schuster)

This book doesn't actually state its setting, but it is by the sea and has architecture that reflects Rhode Island and other New England states. It is the story of a spider and a young woman who live in a boarding house and who support each other in time of need. It is based on an event in the author's life. ◎≈ **General Fiction**

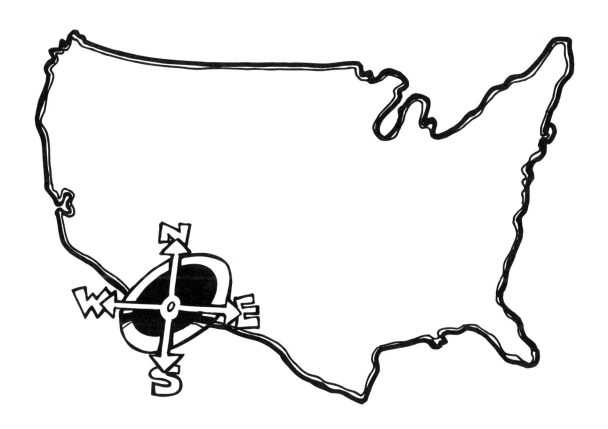

South Carolina

State Flag

Wish You Were Here!

Capital
Columbia

Population
4,012,012

Statehood Date
May 23, 1788

State Number
8th

Motto
While I Breathe, I Hope

Song
"Carolina"

Bird
Carolina Wren

Flower
Yellow Jessamine

Tree
Palmetto

USA

Related State Facts & Trivia

Peculiar Law
It was illegal to file down a mule's teeth.

One of the original 13 states of the Union, South Carolina was the first to secede from the Union before the Civil War.

The 7th president of the United States was Andrew Jackson. He was born on March 4, 1767, in Waxhaw Settlement, South Carolina. After beating the British at the Battle of New Orleans in 1815, he became a national hero.

The state folk dance is the square dance.

In 1830, the first U.S. steam locomotive built for railroad use was put into service in the state.

Literature

All Around Town: The Photographs of Richard Samuel Roberts
by Dinah Johnson
(Henry Holt and Company)

This book chronicles the rich lives of the African American citizens of Columbia, South Carolina, as well as other towns and cities during the 1920s and 1930s. ◎≈ **Historical Nonfiction**

Amber on the Mountain
by Tony Johnston
(Dial Books)

This is a touching story about a little girl who loves her life in the mountains, even though it is lonely. Mountain people live far apart from each other. One day, a friend comes into her life who not only fills the loneliness but changes her life forever by teaching her to read. The book doesn't specify a setting, but it fits into the mountain areas of South Carolina. ◎≈ **General Fiction**

The Firing on Fort Sumter: A Splintered Nation Goes to War
by Nancy A. Colbert
(Morgan Reynolds)

This is a historic tale about the battle that started the American Civil War. ◎≈ **Historical Nonfiction**

The Keeping Room
by Anna Myers
(Walker & Company)

After 13-year-old Joey Kershaw's father leaves to fight in the Revolutionary War, General Cornwallis moves into Charleston and chooses the Kershaw home as his headquarters. ◎≈ **Historical Fiction**

The Wagon
by Tony Johnson
(Tambourine Books)

As the story of a slave family who is freed at the end of the war, this book serves many purposes. It describes the hardships and frustrations of being a slave. It also presents their indescribable relief at being freed at the end of the Civil War and their grief and sadness over the death of Abraham Lincoln. ◎≈ **General Fiction**

South Dakota

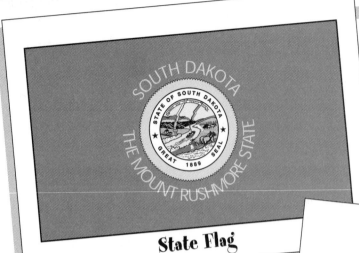

State Flag

SOUTH DAKOTA
THE MOUNT RUSHMORE STATE

Wish You Were Here!

Capital
Pierre

Population
754,844

Statehood Date
November 2, 1889

State Number
40th

Motto
Under God, the People Rule

Song
"Hail, South Dakota"

Bird
Ring-Necked Pheasant

Flower
Pasqueflower

Tree
Black Hills Spruce

USA

Related State Facts & Trivia

Peculiar Law:
It was illegal for an 80-year-old woman to stop in the street to talk to a young married man.

Sitting Bull's grave sits on a bluff overlooking the Missouri River near Mobridge. It wasn't always there. In 1953, under the cover of darkness, a group of South Dakotans snuck into North Dakota, exhumed his bones (with his relatives' permission), and reburied them in their rightful home.

The Prairie Dog, which South Dakota has plenty of, is really a type of squirrel that lives in the ground in large groups known as colonies or towns. They're very social animals who groom each other and appear to kiss. They'll issue loud, barking noises if enemies are near.

Sculptor Gutzon Borglum began drilling into the 5,725-ft (1,745-m) mountain in 1927. The creation of Mount Rushmore, the Shrine of Democracy, took 14 years to complete. The faces are 70 ft (21 m) high.

Literature

The Field Mouse and the Dinosaur Named Sue
by Jan Wahl
(Scholastic)

This is the true story of the discovery of the largest and most complete T-Rex ever found. The setting is the hot and dry hills of South Dakota. The story has an interesting and fun twist to it, as a field mouse who was using one of the bones as a home, goes on a search for it.
◎≈ **Science**

**Kids in Pioneer Times
(Kids Throughout History)**
by Lisa A. Wroble
(Powerkids Press)

This book describes the lives of two students whose family settled on the frontier in what is now South Dakota. The author includes information about their home, clothes, food, and daily activities.
◎≈ **Historical Nonfiction**

Lakota Hoop Dancer
by Jacqueline Left Hand Bull
(Dutton)

The reader follows the activities of Kevin Locke, a Hunkpapa Indian, as he prepares for and performs the traditional Lakota hoop dance. ◎≈ **Information**

Pioneer Girl
by William Anderson
(HarperCollins)

This book begins with the birth of Laura Ingalls Wilder and ends with her death. When Laura is just a little girl, her family makes a move from the little house in the Wisconsin woods. They travel through many states, but they finally settle in De Smet, South Dakota. It's a chronicle of the life of this remarkable woman, who is loved by all.
◎≈ **Biography**

South Dakota: An Alphabetical Scrapbook
by Jodi Holley Latza
(PeopleScapes Inc.)

This handsome book is a fun and exciting way to teach students about South Dakota's infinite variety. It documents the state using the alphabet as a guide, combining beautiful color photography, educational poetry, and interesting facts for a fun reading experience. ◎≈ **Information**

A Year Without Rain
by D. Anne Love
(Holiday House)

Her mother's death and a year-long drought make life difficult for twelve-year-old Rachel and her family on their farm in the Dakotas, but when she learns that her father plans to get married again, it is almost more than Rachel can bear. ◎≈ **Historical Nonfiction**

Tennessee

State Flag

Wish You Were Here!

Capital
Nashville

Population
5,689,283

Statehood Date
June 1, 1796

State Number
16th

Motto
Agriculture and Commerce

USA

Song
"The Tennessee Waltz"

Bird
Mockingbird

Flower
Iris

Tree
Tulip-Poplar

Related State Facts & Trivia

Peculiar Law
It is illegal to sell bologna on Sunday.

Nashville is sometimes called the "Athens of the South" because of an abundance of buildings that copy the Greek style of architecture. The world's only full-scale replica of the Parthenon temple (Athens, Greece) stands in Centennial Park.

Nashville's Grand Ole Opry is the longest continuously running live radio program in the world. It has broadcast every Friday and Saturday night since 1925.

The Cherokee Indian Sequoyah was the only man in history to single-handedly develop and perfect an alphabet. The Sequoyah Birthplace Museum is located in Vonore.

Literature

A Picture Book of Davy Crockett
by David A. Adler
(Holiday House)

The life and times of Davy Crockett are very nicely told in this little book. The tallest tales about this legendary figure were ones he told about himself; yet, determined not to be represented as something he was not, he refused an invitation to Harvard because he was afraid they intended to give him an honorary degree. ◎≋ **Biography**

Swamp Angel
by Anne Isaacs
(Dutton)

This is an original tall tale about a mammoth-sized girl who grows to be the greatest "woodsman" in all of Tennessee. ◎≋ **Legend**

Weaver's Daughter
by Kimberly Brubaker Bradley
(Delacorte Press Books)

In 1791, after her family's journey from Pennsylvania, ten-year-old Lizzie suffers from asthma in her new home in the Southwest Territory (present-day Tennessee). ◎≋ **General Fiction**

Wilma Unlimited
by Kathleen Krull
(Harcourt)

Wilma Rudolph was born in Clarksville, Tennessee, in 1940. She only weighed 4 pounds (2 kg) at birth, and most people believed she wouldn't have a very long life. Before she was five, she contracted polio. She had 19 older brothers and sisters to take care of her and parents who worked very hard, too. This is the story of how she overcame the troubles in her life and became the first woman to win three gold medals in track at a single Olympics. ◎≋ **Biography**

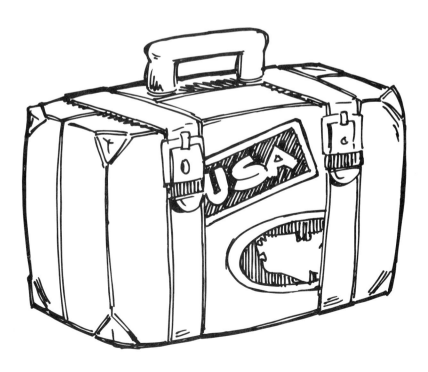

Texas

State Flag

Wish You Were Here!

Capital
Austin

Population
20,851,820

Statehood Date
December 29, 1845

State Number
28th

Motto
Friendship

Song
"Texas, Our Texas"

Bird
Mockingbird

Flower
Bluebonnet

Tree
Pecan

USA

Related State Facts & Trivia

Peculiar Law
It used to be illegal to carry a pair of pliers.

Texas is the country's biggest producer of oil, cattle, sheep, minerals, and cotton.

The Republic of Texas was born in 1836 following the war between American settlers in Texas and the Mexican government. The war included the well known battle of the Alamo. Sam Houston was president of the small republic.

Texas has its own pledge for the state flag: "Honor the Texas Flag; I pledge allegiance to thee, Texas, one and indivisible."

The Texas armadillo is the only armadillo in the U.S. It is also known as the nine-banded armadillo because it is covered with nine thin, bony plates. It eats insects and worms.

Literature

The Armadillo From Amarillo
by Lynne Cherry
(Harcourt)

An armadillo named Sasparillo takes off on a tour of the state of Texas. He ends up traveling on the back of an eagle. He sees many Texas sights and sends postcards to friends along the way. ◎≈ **General Fiction**

Armadillo Rodeo
by Jan Brett
(G. P. Putnam's Sons)

Set in the Texas countryside, an adventurous armadillo mistakes a pair of bright red cowboy boots for a bright red armadillo and follows them to a rodeo. Even though he doesn't get what he thought he was getting, he has a great time at the rodeo. ◎≈ **General Fiction**

Black Cowboy, Wild Horses
by Julius Lester
(Dial Books)

This is the true story of Bob Lemmons who was a former slave. He became a famous Texas cowboy tracker after he became a free man. He was able to connect so well with a herd of mustangs, that he could gain their confidence and bring them in on his own. This book is beautifully illustrated and is great to read aloud. ◎≈ **Biography**

Bubba the Cowboy Prince (A Fractured Texas Tale)
by Helen Ketteman
(Scholastic)

The stepson of a wicked rancher, Bubba, plays the role of Cinderella in this very funny story. It comes complete with two cruel stepbrothers and, of course, a fairy god-cow. ◎≈ **Legends**

Ruby Mae Has Something to Say
by David Small
(Crown)

Ruby Mae lives in the teeny-tiny town of Nada, Texas; however, she has a big dream. She wants to someday speak about world peace at the United Nations in New York City. She has a big problem, though. She has a speech problem. Her nephew invents something to correct her speech, and she ends up at the United Nations. Her dream comes true. ◎≈ **General Fiction**

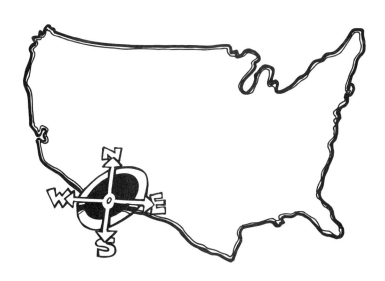

Utah

State Flag

Wish You Were Here!

Capital
Salt Lake City

Population
2,233,169

Statehood Date
January 4, 1896

State Number
45th

Motto
Industry

Song
"Utah, We Love Thee"

Bird
Seagull

Flower
Sego Lily

Tree
Blue Spruce

Related State Facts & Trivia

Peculiar Law
It is illegal not to drink milk.

The bobcat, also known as the lynx, thrives in Utah's mountain forests and rocky terrain. The bobcat generally feeds at night on rodents, rabbits, birds, and sometimes deer.

Mormons, a nickname for members of the Church of Jesus Christ of Latter-Day Saints, settled in Utah and started building Salt Lake City in 1847. They were fleeing religious persecution in the east. The land was dry and salty, so the settlers created a network of irrigation channels to grow crops.

The honeybee became Utah's official state insect in 1983 through the lobbying efforts of a fifth-grade class.

Literature

Cleo and the Coyote
by Elizabeth Levy
(HarperCollins)

Cleo is a stray dog living on the streets in New York City when his life is changed forever. He is found by a little boy and taken home. The boy's family takes a trip to Utah, and this is when the excitement begins. Out in the desert, Cleo gets lost and meets up with a coyote named Tricky. It's a fun story with great illustrations. Each page is bordered in an Indian blanket pattern. ◎≋ **General Fiction**

Iron Horses
by Verla Kay
(G. P. Putnam's Sons)

It's the second half of the nineteenth century, and the race to build a transcontinental railroad is on. The Central Pacific Railroad is coming from the west, and the Union Pacific Railroad is coming from the east. They will meet in Utah. ◎≋ **Historical Nonfiction**

Two Cool Coyotes
by Jillian Lund
(Dutton)

This is a great book about friendship. It not only addresses how much fun it is to have a special friend, but how hard it is to say good-bye to one. It goes a couple of steps further and tells how to fill the empty spaces left by a friend who moves away and how to make a new friend. The book doesn't specify Utah as the setting, but it certainly looks like Utah, which has its fair share of coyote citizens. ◎≋ **General Fiction**

White Water
by Jonathan and
Aaron London
(Viking)

River rafting down the beautiful Green River in Desolation Canyon, Utah, a father and son share an exhilarating experience. It's the boy's first time to ride the white water rapids, and the authors do a great job bringing the story to life. ◎≋ **General Fiction**

Vermont

State Flag

Wish You Were Here!

Capital
Montpelier

Population
608,827

Statehood Date
March 4, 1791

State Number
14th

Motto
Freedom and Unity

Song
"Hail, Vermont"

Bird
Hermit Thrush

Flower
Red Clover

Tree
Sugar Maple

Related State Facts & Trivia

Peculiar Law
It was illegal to paint a horse.

The first constitution to outlaw slavery was Vermont's in 1777.

Vermont makes more maple syrup, marble, and monument granite than any other state. In late winter/early spring, millions of trees are tapped for the annual maple syrup harvest. The sap is sugared down in special buildings where the water in the sap boils off in an evaporator. It takes the sap of four trees to produce 1 gal (3.8 liters) of maple syrup.

The area which is today Vermont was first explored by Frenchman Samuel de Champlain in 1609, when he claimed it for his home country.

Literature

As Long As There Are Mountains
by Natalie Kinsey-Warnock
(Cobblehill/Dutton)

Thirteen-year-old Iris dreams of one day running the family farm in northern Vermont, but the summer of 1956 holds many shocking changes that threaten the life Iris loves. ◎≋ **General Fiction**

At Grandpa's Sugar Bush
by Margaret Carney
(General Distribution Services)

A young boy and his grandfather go into the woods, tap the trees, collect the sap, and turn it into maple syrup to pour on their pancakes. This story is about a boy and his grandpa and, also, about where maple syrup comes from. ◎≋ **General Fiction**

Faraway Summer
by Johanna Hurwitz
(Morrow Junior Books)

In the summer of 1910, Dossi, a poor Russian immigrant from the tenements of New York, spends two weeks with the Meade family on their Vermont farm, and all their lives are enriched by the experience. ◎≋ **General Fiction**

The Mareõs Nest
by Gary Bowen
(HarperCollins)

This book has a mystery to be solved. The setting is the Vermont countryside during the summer of 1846, and something strange is afoot. It involves a wayfaring artist who specializes in portraits of livestock and pets. ◎≋ **General Fiction**

Nearer Nature
by Jim Arnosky
(Lothrop, Lee & Shepard)

The noted naturalist and artist presents sketches and observations from his walks around the Vermont farm where he lives. ◎≋ **Science**

Sugaring Season: Making Maple Syrup
by Diane L. Burns.
(Carolrhoda Books)

This book describes, in text and photographs, the making of maple syrup from tapping the tree and collecting the sap to cooking and packaging it. ◎≋ **Science**

Westminster West
by Jessie Haas
(Greenwillow Books)

Two sisters struggle with their roles as women within the family and within society as an arsonist threatens their post–Civil War Vermont community. ◎≋ **Historical Fiction**

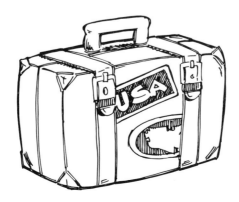

Virginia

State Flag

Wish You Were Here!

Capital
Richmond

Population
7,078,515

Statehood Date
June 25, 1788

State Number
10th

Motto
Thus Always to Tyrants

Song
"Carry Me Back to Old Virginia"

Bird
Cardinal

Flower
Flowering Dogwood

Tree
Dogwood

Related State Facts & Trivia

Peculiar Law
It was illegal to have a bathtub in the house.

Virginia was the site of the surrenders that ended the American Revolution (Yorktown) and the Civil War (Appomattox).

The Blue Ridge Mountains attract many hikers and campers and extend south into North Carolina. They are home to hardwood and conifer forests, bears, deer, bobcats, and 200 species of birds. So many types of flowers flourish in these mountains that they have not all been listed.

U.S. Presidents George Washington, Woodrow Wilson, James Madison, James Monroe, Thomas Jefferson, William Henry Harrison, Zachary Taylor, and John Tyler all hail from Virginia.

Literature

Miz Berlin Walks
by Jane Yolen
(Philomel)

Mary Louise gradually gets to know and love her elderly neighbor lady who tells stories as she walks around the block of her Virginia home. ◎≋ **General Fiction**

Pocahontas: Young Peacemaker (Childhood of Famous Americans Series)
by Leslie Gourse
(Aladdin)

This book examines the life of Pocahontas and how her contact with the English colonists helps to bring trust and friendship with her tribe. ◎≋ **Biography**

The Promise Quilt
by Candice F. Ransom
(Walker and Co.)

After her father leaves the family farm on Lost Mountain to be General Lee's guide, Addie finds ways to remember him—even when he does not return at the end of the Civil War. ◎≋ **Historical Fiction**

Tanya's Reunion
by Valerie Flournoy
(Dial Books)

When she and her grandmother go to help with preparations for a big family reunion, Tanya learns about the history of the farm in Virginia where her grandma grew up. ◎≋ **General Fiction**

Waterman's Boy
by Susan Sharpe
(Bradbury Press)

This is a story of ten-year-old Ben. His father is a waterman on the Chesapeake Bay, and his mother has converted their home into a bed-and-breakfast inn. Ben and his friend help a scientist find the people who are dumping oil into the bay. ◎≋ **General Fiction/Science**

When the Whippoorwill Calls
by Candice F. Ransom
(Tambourine Books)

A Blue Ridge Mountain family is displaced to the flatlands by the creation of the Shenandoah National Park. ◎≋ **Historical Fiction**

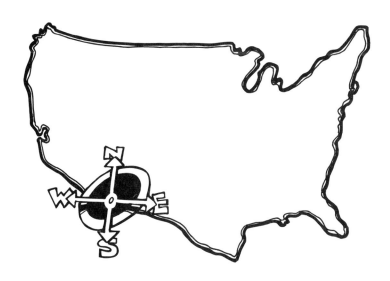

Washington

State Flag

Wish You Were Here!

Capital
Olympia

Population
5,894,121

Statehood Date
November 11, 1889

State Number
42nd

Motto
By and By

Song
"Washington, My Home"

Bird
American Goldfinch

Flower
Rhododendron

Tree
Western Hemlock

Related State Facts & Trivia

Peculiar Law
It was illegal to hunt ducks from a rowboat unless one were upright and visible from the waist up.

Mt. St. Helens erupted on May 18, 1980, with the force of an atomic bomb after lying dormant for 123 years. Sixty people died in the explosion and ash covered hundreds of miles of surrounding land and forests.

The Green Darner Dragonfly, also known as the "mosquito hawk," is the state insect. This dragonfly can be found throughout Washington and is a beneficial contributor to the ecosystem because it consumes a large number of insect pests.

Washington is number one in the country in the production of these fruits and vegetables: apples, lentils, dry edible peas, hops, pears, red raspberries, spearmint oil, and sweet cherries. It is the leading apple producer in the country, especially the red and golden delicious varieties.

Literature

Bluebird Summer
by Deborah Hopkinson
(Greenwillow Books)

A young girl and her brother find that the summer visit to their grandparents' farm just isn't the same since Grandma died. Will Grandpa ever be happy again? The little girl, Mags, works hard on a project, bringing back the things that Grandma loved and finds that it brings a big change in Grandpa. According to the author, the bluebirds pictured in the book are Eastern bluebirds, but the story was inspired by her observations of Western bluebirds near her home in Washington state. ◎≋ **General Fiction**

Brother Eagle, Sister Sky paintings
by Susan Jeffers
(Dial Books)

Much of the text of this beautifully illustrated book comes from a speech by Chief Seattle, a Suquamish Indian. His speech was given more than 100 years ago, and it is about his people's love of the earth and their concern about protecting it. Historians have different opinions about the origins of this speech, and some believe it is actually a letter. The message of the book is the same, regardless of the origin of the words. ◎≋ **Historical Nonfiction**

Double Trouble in Walla Walla
by Andrew Clements
(The Millbrook Press)

It's an ordinary Monday in Walla Walla, Washington, until Lulu raises her hand in class and discovers that she is in some kind of a word warp. Before she knows it, her teacher, the principal, and the school nurse are all suffering from the same language problem. ◎≋ **General Fiction**

A Green Horn Blowing
by David F. Birchman
(Lothrop Lee & Shepard)

This story is set during the Great Depression, and although the author doesn't specify the location, it is on a berry farm much like the one he grew up on in Battle Ground, Washington. It's a moving story about a young boy who builds a friendship with a farmhand who teaches him how to play the trombolia (a squash that is shaped like a trombone). ◎≋ **Historical Fiction**

West Virginia

State Flag

Capital
Charleston

Population
1,808,344

Statehood Date
June 20, 1863

State Number
35th

Motto
Mountaineers Are
Always Free

Song
"The West Virginia Hills"

Bird
Cardinal

Flower
Rhododendron

Tree
Sugar Maple

Related State Facts & Trivia

Peculiar Law
Only babies can ride in a baby carriage.

Grave Creek Mound in Moundsville, West Virginia, is one of the largest Native American burial mounds. Relics there date as far back as the first century B.C.

West Virginia was a part of Virginia until that state seceded from the United States in 1861. Delegates from 40 counties formed their own government, and statehood was granted them two years later.

Harpers Ferry witnessed the first successful application of interchangeable manufacture, the arrival of the first successful American railroad, John Brown's attack on slavery, the largest surrender of federal troops during the Civil War, and the education of former slaves in one of the earliest integrated schools in the United States.

Literature

John Henry
by Julius Lester
(Dial Books)

This is a fictionalized account of the legend about John Henry, an ex-slave who supposedly worked on the Chesapeake and Ohio Railroad in the 1870s. The competition between John Henry (that steel driving man) and the steam drill reportedly occurred in the Big Bend Tunnel in the Allegheny Mountains in Summers County, West Virginia. ◎≈ **Legend**

The Rag Coat
by Lauren Mills
(Little, Brown and Company)

Minna's family is very poor and lives in the Appalachian Mountains. More than anything, she wants to be able to go to school. What prevents her is the fact that she doesn't have a coat to wear. When the quilting mothers of the area get together and make her one, she doesn't expect the reaction she gets from the kids at school. This is a book with lessons, inspired by the songs and stories from Appalachia. Because of the connection to coal mining, it fits nicely into a study of West Virginia. ◎≈ **General Fiction**

Shiloh
by Phyllis Reynolds Naylor
(Atheneum Books)

When he finds a lost beagle in the hills behind his West Virginia home, Marty tries to hide it from his family and the dog's real owner, a mean-spirited man known to shoot deer out of season and to mistreat his dogs. ◎≈ **General Fiction**

Silver Packages
by Cynthia Rylant
(Orchard Books)

Each year since 1943, a very special train has traveled through Appalachia, bringing happiness to the many students who wait along the tracks for it. They call it the Santa Train. This book is a fictionalized account of this special train. ◎≈ **Historical Fiction**

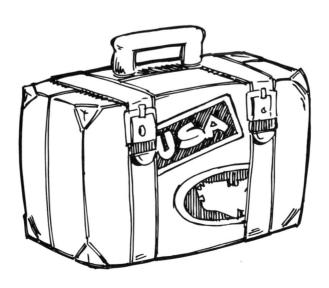

Wisconsin

WISCONSIN

FORWARD

1848

State Flag

Wish You Were Here!

Capital
Madison

Population
5,363,675

Statehood Date
May 29, 1848

State Number
30th

Motto
Forward

Song
"On, Wisconsin"

Bird
Robin

Flower
Purple Violet

Tree
Sugar Maple

Related State Facts & Trivia

Peculiar Law
For each meal sold costing 25 cents or more, a small piece of cheese had to be served.

The mourning dove (Zenaidura macrour) was named the state symbol of peace in 1971 following a decade of statewide debate.

Wisconsin has more milk cows (1,500,000) than any other state and produces over 15% of the entire country's milk. Of the 80,000 farms, over half are geared to dairying, and the state is nick-named "America's Dairyland."

Wisconsin has over 14,000 lakes. Lake Winnebago is the largest. The state also has 7,446 streams and rivers. If you placed them end to end, they'd stretch nearly 27,000 mi (43,450 km) — enough to circle the whole planet.

Literature

Century Farm: One Hundred Years on a Family Farm
by Cris Peterson
(Boyds Mills Press)

The story of a 100-year-old family farm in Wisconsin is told in photographs and in anecdotes about the three generations of people who have owned and farmed the land. ◎≋ **Information**

Cranberries: Fruit of the Bogsby
by Diane L. Burns
(Carolrhoda Books)

In this photo book, students will learn the history of cranberries and then visit a modern cranberry farm through the seasons. ◎≋ **Science**

Hank Aaron— Brave in Every Way
by Peter Golenbock
(Harcourt)

This is an inspirational story about Hank Aaron's climb to success as the Baseball Hall of Famer who, on April 8, 1974, broke Babe Ruth's home run record. His dream to play baseball on a National League team began when he was a little boy in Alabama. It came true in 1954, when the Milwaukee Braves signed him on as a player. ◎≋ **Biography**

Little House in the Big Woods
by Laura Ingalls Wilder
(HarperTrophy)

This chapter book is the story of the Wilder family's life in the Wisconsin Woods before they moved out onto the prairie.
◎≋ **General Fiction**

Right Here on This Spot
by John Clapp
(Houghton Mifflin)

While digging a ditch in his cabbage field, Grandpa uncovers various items that provide clues to what has happened in that area of Wisconsin from the time of the Ice Age to the twentieth century.
◎≋ **Science**

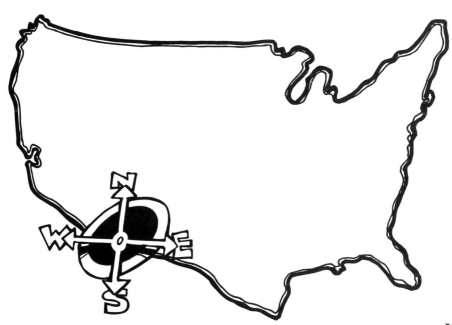

Wyoming

State Flag

Wish You Were Here!

Capital
Cheyenne

Population
493,782

Statehood Date
July 10, 1890

State Number
44th

Motto
Equal Rights

Song
"Wyoming"

Bird
Western Meadowlark

Flower
Indian Paintbrush

Tree
Cottonwood

USA

Related State Facts & Trivia

Peculiar Law

A license was required to take a picture of a rabbit during January, February, March, or April.

The bison was adopted as the state mammal on February 23, 1985.

Established on March 1, 1872, Yellowstone National Park is the first and oldest national park in the world. The park includes 10,000 geysers, as well as hot springs, mud volcanoes, fossil forests, and several canyons and waterfalls. Wolves were reintroduced in Yellowstone in 1995.

In 1925, Mrs. Nellie Tayloe Ross was elected to succeed her late husband as governor of Wyoming and became the first woman governor in the United States. She was later appointed director of the U.S. Mint.

Literature

Ridin' That Strawberry Roan
by Marcia Sewall
(Viking Kestrel)

Based on an old Western folk song, this book tells the story of a brave but foolhardy bronc buster. This cowboy finally meets his match in a very tough horse to ride, the "Strawberry Roan." It's as fun to sing as it is to read. There is no mention of a particular location, but it fits very nicely into the terrain and cowboy culture of Wyoming. ◎≈ **Legend**

The Sweetwater Run
by Andrew Glass
(Doubleday Books)

This is the story of Buffalo Bill Cody and his experiences as a teenage rider for the Pony Express. It is wild and exciting and focuses on a section of the trail between Fort Laramie and Fort Bridger, Wyoming. The ride in this story involves the election results of Abraham Lincoln. ◎≈ **Historical Nonfiction**

Wolves in Yellowstone
by Randy Houk
(Benefactory)

Written in verse, this book tells about a family of wolves in Yellowstone National Park in Wyoming. The book is co-sponsored by the Humane Society of the United States, which encourages animal and environmental protection awareness in young students. ◎≈ **Science**

Yellowstone National Park
by David Petersen
(Children's Press)

This unique book presents all the sights of Yellowstone and includes information that will be highly interesting to students. ◎≈ **Information**

Unit Outline

State _____

Unit Dates: _____

Planned Literature	
Notes:	
Key Vocabulary:	

Center 1	**Center 2**
_____	_____
Materials	**Materials**

Center 3	**Center 4**
_____	_____
Materials	**Materials**